Praise for The Teacher & The Admin

The Teacher & The Admin, written by Gary Armida and Kris Felicello, reminds us how we can make schools better for kids when teachers and administration work together. The authors identify specific challenges facing schools today, offer practical strategies from each perspective, and provide insight how teachers and administration can be better for one another. Filled with reflections from educators in the field, this book will be a big hit with all educators!

~ Jimmy Casas
Educator, Author, Speaker, & Leadership Coach

Thought provoking and eye opening perspectives on the fundamental components of our beloved profession from both a teacher and admin's view! Kris and Gary drive their points home by sharing personal experiences on topics we educators deal with on a daily basis. The lesson the Teacher and the Admin teaches us is that while instructional paradigms are ever changing, one thing remains consistent to always put #kidsfirst!

~ Elaine Alden, Ed. D.
Instructional Mathematics Coach, Benjamin Franklin Elementary School

The Teacher & The Admin demonstrate a compelling example of collaboration. Their mission to implement systematic change in ways that benefit students is innovative and inspirational.

~ Danielle Lauro
Literacy Specialist, & TEDx Curator

If you work with children you must read what The Teacher & The Admin have to share. Their stories are real and their advice is practical. The teacher and the admin inspire educators to be better, think differently, and, most importantly, put kids first. Their drive and passion is effortless!

~ Laura Sweeney
Assistant Principal, Stony Point Elementary School

D0910380

Gary and Kris continue to write real, relevant, vulnerable pieces that open up the importance of leading with vulnerability while helping us all to see how the power in working together for students. Their open, honest stories resonate with all educators. From homework, grading, and feedback to valuing the voices of students and staff and more, the real examples and human side of leadership truly comes through. As a coordinator of professional learning the topics in this book will help guide my conversations with teachers and leaders as we learn and grow together this year.

~ Katie Macfarlene
Director of Professional Development, &
Co-founder @edcampFLX @EdCamp_URWarner #CoffeeEDUROC

The Teacher & The Admin beautifully tackles multiple ways schools and districts can move forward with all stakeholders working hand-in-hand. The topics, to which any educator could relate, appropriately include: parent involvement, student voice, professional learning, and more. Practical tips and action steps are provided throughout, and the many revealing stories resonate with me on so many levels. Most uniquely, to feature multiple perspectives, each chapter contains a section written by The Teacher and a section written by The Admin. Highly recommended!

~ Ross Cooper
Elementary Assistant Principal, Chappaqua Central School District, &
Author of Hacking Project Based Learning

What does it take to make schools a better place for kids? Teacher Gary Armida and Assistant Superintendent Kris Felicello provide key takeaways from their years of experience in education. By uniquely including the voice of the teacher and an administrator plus "voices from the field" this book provides deeper insight into the world of education and is a great resource for everyone who is interested in making schools a better place for kids.

~ Denise Murai
Parent & Community Liaison at Hahaione Elementary, Honolulu, HI,
& HundrED Ambassador

Kris and Gary's gift of storytelling coupled with their unflinching honesty make this book a must read for both teachers and administrators. Unlike most books, The Teacher & The Admin takes you on a journey from beginning to end. This is not a highlight reel full of advice but rather a chronicle of two educators' journeys that shares the good and the bad of their careers. As you read The Teacher and the Admin you feel as if you are learning with them not from them."

~ Jon Harper
Author of My Bad: 24 Educators Who Messed Up, Fessed Up and Grew!; Host of My Bad, & Co-Host of Teachers Aid Podcasts featured on Bam radio

The Teacher & The Admin is a masterful and transparent journey of two perspectives, which serve the same goal - building relationships to change the lives of students. Kris and Gary share inspiring stories of their trials to transform the role of education and push the boundaries of traditional practices. Our schools provide so much more than tests, homework, and grades. Throughout the book, I gained practical and tangible practices to enhance my skills as an educator. The Teacher & the Admin will be a useful resource to many teachers and administrators!

~ Joshua Stamper
Administrator, Blogger, & Host of Aspire: The Leadership Development Podcast

Typically, when we talk about how to provide students with a "better" education than they are getting in today's schools, the conversation centers around improving academics, raising test scores, more advanced placement courses, and increasingly competitive college acceptances. In their inspiring book, The Teacher & The Admin: Making Schools Better for Kids, Gary Armida (the teacher) and Kris Felicello (the admin), invite us to challenge the status quo when it comes to improving schools for students. Drawing upon their personal and professional experiences as teachers, administrators, parents, and learners, they offer practical suggestions for building better relationships among students and educators, making parents feel more welcome in their children's schools, and giving students more choice and voice in growing their talents and interests.

~ Ellen Feig Gray
Parent Educator, Coach, Founder of Parent with Perspective, & Co-Author of Hacking School Culture: Designing Compassionate Classrooms

The Teacher & The Admin offers a REVOLUTIONARY format delivered with a refreshing mix of practicality and educational artistry. As Armida and Felicello share their INSPIRED perspectives about some of the most critical aspects within the learning environment, readers invariably discover how differing positions help form the EMPOWERED partnership to unlock educational excellence. This is simply TOP-NOTCH literature that pushes thinking, reflecting, and ultimately enhances collegial empathy. It's the type of book that one refers back to again and again, in their pursuit of mastery. Highest recommendation possible!

~ Hans Appel
Middle School Counselor & Creator of Award Winning Culture

The Teacher & The Admin is a book that NEEDED to be written. Felicello & Armida hit on topics that all educators need to hear. Education will not work unless the teacher and the admin understand one's intentions, direction and responsibility. This book makes those three standards oh so clear for all ears. A must read for all education staff members.

~ Joe "Mr. D" Dombrowski
Elementary Educator, Speaker & Advocate

Throw a rock, and it will land on a new education book that promises solutions to our greatest problems in education. There are many self-professed experts out there and quite a few whose research has earned them that distinction. This book is different, and it's different because Kris and Gary are different. I've had the privilege of working and learning and problem solving beside them often in recent years, and their willingness to reflect and practice humility with great intention not only inspired me--it helped everyone move forward. Read this book not for the direction it provides, but for the wisdom you will gain simply by hearing Gary and Kris's stories. They're experienced practitioners whose work has made them increasingly human.

~ Angela Stockman
Author, Teacher, & Professional Learning Service Provider

Filled with personal stories & practical strategies from two different perspectives in the education field, The Teacher & The Admin have created a #kidsfirst resource for both administrators and teachers illustrating positive changes that can occur when a culture of collaboration is nurtured."

~ Reyna Texler
Ruby Sneakers Consulting LLC

Kris and Gary have created a book that shares the variety of views between teachers and administrators to create a truly awesome learning community. The book will surely help all stakeholders gain needed insight and perspective about building better school communities.

~ Starr Sackstein
Author & Educational Consultant

Finally! A collaboration of voice and forward looking ideas from a teacher and an administrator. This book should be required reading for anyone looking to make their school better for kids. Smart, witty, and relatable.

~ Kleo Girandola
Supervisor Mathematics & Data Driven Instruction at Rockland BOCES

The Teacher & The Admin is a game changer for anyone considering taking the leap into school administration. Authors Armida and Felicello are transparent and share from their personal experiences and leave the reader with valuable takeaways at the end of each chapter. This is a book I wish I had access to at the beginning of my administrative journey!

~ Basil Martin
Assistant Principal, DeKalb County Schools, GA

THE TEACHER & THE ADMIN

MAKING SCHOOLS BETTER FOR KIDS

KRIS FELICELLO & GARY ARMIDA

To Em--Dreams actually do come true.
To Mom and Dad--You were right.
To Krystal--Thank you for being My Person.
To my fellow teachers--I am proud to be in this profession with you.
To my students--Thank you.
GA

To my boys- You teach me everyday.
To Rebecca- You are the love of my life.
To my mother- Thank you for always being my biggest fan.
To my parents-Thank you for always believing in me.
To all those I have worked with- Thank you for the lessons learned.
To all the kids I served- I hope I helped at least a little bit.
KF

CONTENTS

INTRO FROM THE ADMIN

Dr. Kris Felicello

I was driving home from the Schools to Watch Conference (STW) with Gary (AKA The Teacher), feeling pretty good. My good friend Anthony and his school, Fieldstone Middle School, were recognized as a 'Schools to Watch School". I was proud of my friend's and my District's accomplishment. I was also proud that I had played a small part in making Fieldstone what it is today.

Equally thrilling was when Gary and I introduced ourselves to one of our heroes in education, Rick Wormeli. I have been reading his books and following his work for as long I can remember. In fact, I still have my autographed copy of Meet Me in the Middle that my mentor Paul had given to me when I was named middle school principal over 15 years ago.

I tried to be confident and not too starstruck and remembered a phrase that Anthony uses often, "act like you have been there before."

This became increasingly difficult when Rick actually knew who we were and told us our blog was currently his favorite! When he said my writing was eloquent, the smile of disbelief on my face could not be contained. Rick went on to tell us that we should write a book, and he even shouted us out in his keynote presentation. When Rick Wormeli tells you to write a book, you listen!

Gary and I decided to use our time driving back to New York from DC to outline the first of hopefully many The Teacher and The Admin books for educators. We bounced around a few ideas for titles, topics, and format and ultimately landed with the structure you hold in your hands today, topics that we feel can make schools better for kids.

Each chapter tackles the issue from the teacher's perspective and from the administrator's perspective; the thought being when teachers and administrators work together, schools get better and kids benefit. To make schools the institutions of learning that students deserve, all educators must be dedicating themselves to improve.

How is that done? What does that look like from two different perspectives? These are some of the questions we hope to provide some, but not all, of the answers to.

Ultimately, our goal is to get educators thinking, creating, building trust, and doing things better. The day you decide you are good enough and no longer need to improve, is, in my mind, the day it is time to hang them up and retire. Trying new things, looking for a different approach, improving practice, does not mean you were doing it wrong before; it just means you want to do it better. Lebron James, the best basketball player on the planet, doesn't stop trying to get better, even after 15 years of success in the league. Authors don't stop trying to write a better book even after publishing a best seller. Doctors, lawyers, politicians, businessmen, and engineers alike are always striving to improve their craft. And, if they don't, they will quickly find themselves irrelevant.

Should educators be any different?

I hope my best day as an educator is my last because if I am not improving and growing, then I feel I am doing my kids and the field I love a disservice. It was only when I started to stare at my mistakes right in the face and learn from them did I really start to grow into an educator who is an asset to the field. It's painful and embarrassing sometimes, easier to ignore and forget, yet I know true growth comes when we embrace our mistakes and learn from them.

So, no, I don't claim to have all the answers nor will this book provides you with all of them. But, I am optimistic that it will give you some insights into what I have learned from my mistakes and encourage you to learn from yours as well.

INTRO FROM THE TEACHER

Gary Armida

There was a time when I didn't really think I should be a teacher. Actually, if I am honest, there were multiple times. The first time was when I was in college. I was finishing up my junior year and I panicked a bit. After doing my observation hours, I wasn't sure if I could be that guy every single day. So, I went to my advisor and asked if I could still graduate with my English Degree. He laid out a plan and that's what happened. I had a great, memorable senior year and then graduated.

I got a job right out of school, working for a rental car company. I immediately knew I made a big mistake. The whole corporate life thing wasn't for me. I wanted to quit, but felt that I would truly be a failure if I quit my first job, especially after making the decision to quit pursuing teaching right before student teaching. But, the universe would throw me a big sign. I was asked to go pick up a gentleman and bring him to the office so he can get his rental car. The man entered the car and immediately struck up a conversation. He began telling me about how he had just retired after 35 years as a teacher.

Talk about a sign.

I told him that I had started out as wanting to be a teacher, but had bailed before the last step. He didn't tell me I made a mistake, but he did tell me this: "I had a wonderful life because I made the decision to be a teacher. I raised my family and spent 35 years trying to help kids. What more could a man want?"

I think he could tell that his words hit home with me as I drove silently for a few minutes. He interrupted the silence with "You're young. There is still time. I am sure you will make a lot more money doing this, but if your heart isn't into it, find something where your heart wants to be."

I quit the next day and re-enrolled at my college. 21 years later, I can safely say that it was the best decision I've made in my professional life.

I thought about leaving education one more time, about 10 years in, as I began writing sports and making small, but decent headway into that industry. But, the universe did its thing again.

Rick Peterson, a former Major League Baseball Pitching Coach, became a friend after we worked on some writing pieces together. He always told me that he thought I was doing great, meaningful work because I was a teacher. One day he said, "It is a privilege of a lifetime to make a difference in the lives of others."

That's what teaching is.

That mindset has helped me enjoy my entire 21 years in the classroom, especially lately. Teaching isn't a repetitive thing; the good ones do different things every year. Each year there are new people to impact with new, innovative lessons. We can inspire, we can help kids question the world and develop enough confidence to find complicated solutions to even more complicated problems.

I knew I had an ally the instant I met The Admin. In our first meeting, Kris spoke passionately about wanting to make schools better for kids. He backed up his words with action, making the jump to central office after reforming our middle school in one year. At central, he has had the courage to lead many initiatives that have led or will lead to real change that will benefit our students. Yet, he is still in the classrooms with kids, still giving professional development opportunities for everyone, and still wants to do more.

As it turned out, he is a pretty good guy and we became friends. Yes, a teacher and an administrator can actually be friends. One day I mentioned to him that I might start writing about education. He immediately asked if he could too. A few weeks later, we started the Teacher and The Admin site.

I was surprised at how quickly things went for us. Districts asked if they could use our articles for their professional development sessions. Education leaders such as Rick Wormeli and Alfie Kohn complimented our work and pushed it through social media. And, as Kris said, Rick Wormeli even said that we should write a book.

That drive back from the Schools to Watch Conference was another one of those universe moments. We had talked about writing a book together, but those six hours of driving and talking made it real. We wanted the book to be practical and to show that teachers and administrators can work together and make real change that will help kids. As we planned the format, I got even more excited, even hitting the brakes a bit too hard for The Admin's taste a few times. But, here is the result, a book that we are proud of.

I am proud of the work we have done. Through the site and through the pushing of The Admin, I have connected with people who are changing education. Our voices are in that fight and I am proud of that. This book is the next step. As Kris said, it won't have all the answers. That's not our intent. Through all of the universe pushes, I have realized my experiences and every lesson I have learned can help other teachers. By sharing the good, the bad, the ugly, and the truly nasty-ugly, we can help teachers and educators. Because of that, we are helping more kids.

That is, indeed, a privilege.

1

Building Trust

"Good teams become great ones when the members trust each other enough to surrender the me for the we." ~Phil Jackson

It is not random that the opening chapter of our first educational book is based on trust. We often have intense conversations about ways to improve schools, to change what is antiquated, and to enlighten others in our field to what we believe to be a truth; We can do better for our kids.

True progress, true growth, cannot flourish and take hold without a belief that we are in this together. Trust between administration and teachers does not mean that you will always agree or that you will not become angry with one another, that mistakes won't happen.

What it does mean is that you have a common belief that decisions will be made on what is in the best interest of students, that you will listen, respect, and be honest with one another. This chapter is probably the most important in the book. By sharing stories of what has worked and what hasn't .

Our intent is that you will walk away with the understanding that we are in this together and when we are, we can change lives.

The Admin

When Gary and I first started brainstorming chapters for this book, it was easy to rattle off several areas that we felt schools could better serve kids. Homework, innovation, grading, student voice, choice, conformity, the list got longer and longer when Gary finally said, "you know, none of this works without a level of trust between administration and faculty."

That prompted stories about good leaders and poor leaders; we debated whether the building trust part should be its own chapter or the intro to the book. Since we were driving home from the Schools to Watch conference, the topic of Fieldstone came up. Fieldstone was the middle school in our District that had just received the STW designation. It was also the school I was principal during our District's transformation when we closed two schools, reconfigured our attendance lines, and reimagined Fieldstone from an 8/9 Center to a 7/8 Middle School to house the 1,300 students in a team centered middle-level approach.

My year at Fieldstone was one of my most challenging, yet most rewarding years in education. Passing the torch to the current Principal, Anthony, and seeing him lead the school to this national designation filled me with pride and nostalgia.

Gary asked me some excellent thought-provoking questions, a skill this master teacher has perfected with not only his students.

"What was your vision for the school when you took over?"

I thought for a moment, brought myself back in time and then remembered my "why" from 2012. I wanted Fieldstone a place where kids were excited to go, a place where parents wanted to send their children, and a place where teachers wanted to be. My desire was a building with a family feel, one in which risks were encouraged, one where students, teachers, and custodians broke from the norm. I kept going and going, including all the ideas I was never able to implement because of the opportunity to take a position in central office.

Gary loved my idea for a parent welcome center. A comfortable space for parents as they waited for a meeting or to pick up their child. The welcome room would have a coffee machine, magazines, comfortable seating, and even a place for parents to charge their cell phones. Unfortunately, I ran out of time and this idea never materialized but ultimately our staff embraced the type of environment I had envisioned.

Gary congratulated me and said that "Fieldstone is a great school. Kids can't wait to go, teachers request to be transferred there, and parents never want their kids to leave."

I reminded him that it had been six years since I was principal and Fieldstone was now in the hands of an inspirational leader. Yet, it still made me smile to think about how far Fieldstone had come from the days when High School teachers were moved there and saw it as a punishment.

His next question once again got me thinking, but brought a tinge of guilt to my belly.

"How were you able to get the staff to buy in? Especially since they had seen so many leaders come and go, and they knew you had your sight set on central?"

I felt guilty for leaving them, but that quickly faded when I thought of the amazing leader that took over for me. I knew Gary's perception that I was instantly revered and able to get the staff to believe in me, trust me, and follow me from the get-go was not completely accurate. I made so many mistakes in the early going that by November I had a grievance filed against me for the first time in my administrative career. In the grievance, I was referred to as "Dictatorial Leader whose non-collaborative "my way or the highway" style was hurting the morale of the school and its teachers."

Wow, what a kick in the gut!

What did I do when I first read those words? I got in the car and blasted

"Never Enough" by Eminem. After a few rounds of this song I convinced myself I could take them all on, they couldn't beat me. In essence, I channeled my inner anger. I am happy to say that a teacher I trusted was able to talk some sense into me. She put things in perspective for me and explained that once they know you have their back they will run through a wall for you. I started to reflect and thought back to where I went wrong.

My first blunder occurred on opening day. This is a day where the entire District comes together (650 certificated staff) at our High School. This particular year we had members of our High School band playing a unique piece on modified garbage pails. The first day is filled with excitement; it is an excellent opportunity to reconnect with friends, catch up with colleagues you had worked with in years past, and kiss every single person you see. This is the North Rockland way; you see someone you haven't seen in more than a day, you greet them with a smile, a hug, and a kiss.

This North Rockland tradition was hard for me to acclimate to. I am not a big kisser. It's not that I am afraid of germs, it just seems like an inconvenience at times. Who do you kiss? When do you kiss them? Are they offended if you do, or don't? Sometimes it's a bit awkward, but we are North Rocklanders and we are warm people. I have gotten used to it and, in fact, overuse the kiss like the rest of our community.

Most people are relaxed and happy on the day, but I was a bit on edge. I was scheduled to have my new faculty for about 20 minutes in the High School cafeteria, after which I would escort my new team into the auditorium in our assigned section as our Superintendent addressed her tribe. The previous March I had provided the teachers, who we anticipated would be the new Fieldstone Middle School, with a full day professional learning session, complete with team building activities, explanation of the master schedule, Middle School instruction, team, collaboration and more. It was and remains one of the best sessions I have ever run. I felt like the majority of the teachers left inspired and motivated to make Fieldstone a great place for kids. I had also spent a lot of time in the building planning rooms, offices, and holding informal conversations during that year and, of course, over the summer.

This first day felt different though. It felt more real; this was my first day as their official principal. I had a little tingling in my stomach as I walked to the front of the room. A bit of self-doubt started to form.

Would all of these teachers listen to me?
What would I do if they talked when I did?
Would they take me seriously?
Will I be able to lead a building of over 1,300 students?

Then, I did what I had heard most courageous people do in these situations. I held my head high and faked confidence. Faking it until you make it often works wonders; smile until you are happy, be nice even when you feel anger, be strong even when you feel weak. In fact, Dr. Amy Cuddy from Harvard Business School has conducted studies[1] that have indicated that by just changing your body posture you can evoke a sense of confidence in yourself and in how others see you. The problem on this day was that I wasn't portraying a lack of confidence, but rather the opposite.

I was telling them the way it was going to be - so sure about what I was saying that I forgot about how I was making the audience feel. I was their new leader, in a new building, with a new schedule, new configuration, a whole new set of rules. Because of my anxiety, I forgot that they may have had some too. I talked about all of my expectations. Arrive on time, be in the hallways, turn in paperwork on time, be professional, return all phone calls and emails, and--the one that put them over the top--you must stay until the last bus leaves.

I left the meeting feeling pretty good.

Everyone sat attentively, no one questioned my rules, in essence, everyone had conformed to what they were supposed to do. I had treated them exactly the opposite of how I wanted our kids treated, exactly the opposite of what I felt schools should be about. Were any of my expectations unreasonable? Absolutely not, but was following my rules the most important message I wanted to deliver to my staff on the first day as their official leader? What did that say about our school, my philosophy, how I felt about them?

---

1 "Power Posing: Brief Nonverbal Displays Affect Neuroendocrine Levels and Risk Tolerance." Journal of Research in Crime and Delinquency, journals.sagepub.com/doi/full/10.1177/0956797610383437.

THE **TEACHER** & THE **ADMIN**

Looking back, I realize that I was perpetuating exactly what I am fighting against today. I do not want a school of conformity based on the factory model. I want schools to be places that embrace uniqueness, accentuate different strengths, put students and adults in positions to be successful. Learning that is intrinsic and not based on fear or the promise of a golden ticket.

It took me a long time and a lot of growth to fully understand that I was not the type of leader I wanted to be that day. Rather than building trust, I was building fear. My initial reaction was to point the finger. How could someone argue with high expectations? What kind of people am I charged with leading? Has our profession gotten so entitled that the teachers run to the union because the boss asks them to be on time? It took me a lot of soul searching and certainly a great deal of professional growth to understand how wrong my approach was. Looking back, I wish I had done things differently.

I could have passed out index cards with different TV characters on them and asked the staff to find their matches. Once they found their partner they could have interviewed them based on questions like:

> ? What unique strengths do you have that can help to make our school a special place?
> ? Share a time you made a difference in a child's life?
> ? What are you most excited about?
> ? What fears do you have coming into the year?

I could have been honest and told them my dreams for our school, my fears, my vision, my insecurities.

I could have had them line up in birthday order without speaking.

I could have had table groups share a picture on their phone and why it was a fond memory.

There were a million things I could have done to inspire my staff, to let them know we were on the same team, to get them laughing and having fun. Setting the tone for the type of school I would want my own children to attend.

Anything would have been better than giving them my list of rules. I made them feel exactly how I don't want them to make our students feel.

The grievance forced me to look back and analyze why did my new staff not follow me like my staff at Farley (my previous school in the same District)? I thought about my time at Farley and realized although I had worked hard to establish a positive culture at Fieldstone, I hadn't spent as much time cultivating relationships and explaining the thinking behind the tremendous number of changes I would be making.

When I had first been named principal at Farley I invited each and every staff member to meet with me individually during the summer. This was an excellent opportunity to listen, to learn, to garner a pulse on the building and what made it tick. I met with union leadership, I met with cafeteria, custodial, secretarial staff. I took the time to get to know people, to get to know the school and for them to get to know me. When I was first named principal at Farley I was searching for answers to what the building needed to be successful.

The difference at Fieldstone was that I felt I had all the answers and because of previous success the teachers should follow me. I started to realize what we often do as we get older, the more we learn, the more we learn how little we actually know. I started to understand that I need to listen more, demand less, inspire my staff, and let them know that when push came to shove, I had their backs.

I started doing the things that had helped me develop trust in the past. I made those phone calls, sent those text messages when people were sick or were dealing with a difficult personal situation. I learned more about families, about passions, about common interests. I committed to sending positive emails when I saw good things happening in the classroom. I tried to be more about people and less about the program. The staff noticed the difference and let me know they felt the shift. I had made the declaration to be more collaborative in faculty meetings. I was brutally honest and let the faculty know I want a great school; I knew we could be a great school, but only if we trusted each other. And, to get there, I needed to change.

Things were starting to improve and even the most reluctant were starting to believe and become more positive, more kid-centered. I continued to cultivate my faculty meetings and made them about collaboration, about us learning from each other, rather than me preaching from my PowerPoint pulpit.

One meeting I asked them to bring a recent lesson plan they were proud of and share it at their table. As a group, they would make suggestions for improvements. In another meeting, everyone wrote on the outside of a paper bag something they were struggling with. The bag made its way around the room with each person putting an index card in the bag with a possible solution.

It was at the holiday party when I realized that we were no longer just a faculty, but we were turning into a family. A teacher who I had worked with at Farley congratulated me. I must have looked confused, so the teacher elaborated.

"People are really feeling good about our school and proud of what we are doing. They aren't afraid to make a mistake because they know you will have their back."

This conversation made me realize it is about people, it is about kids, it is about looking after your school family just as you would your home family. I truly believe that schools can be transformed into magical learning places, but only when there is a mutual trust between the staff members regardless of titles. When we embrace each other's "weird", when we are honest, and learn from our mistakes. When the staff trusts each other, we can then earn the trust that is most important in any school, the trust of the students.

The Teacher

On the very first day of my teaching career, I was pulled into an after-work meeting with a bunch of other new hires. The building union representatives wanted to meet with us and give us the lowdown of our rights and responsibilities. The meeting was largely positive as many of the representatives talked about entering a great profession. They gave us the "real" scoop about taking those personal days and sick days that we were told about during our district orientation. For the most part, everyone seemed like they were passionate about the profession and really proud of the middle school that they built. I remember thinking that I wanted to be like them one day.

Then, the head building rep came up to speak. He was fire and brimstone. He was the "watch your back" type of guy. Everyone is out to get you. You could be fired at a moment's notice, but he and the union were there to protect us. It certainly got my attention. Then, he concluded with one last thought that I still remember these 21 years later.

"Never, ever, trust an administrator. They don't know what it's like to be a teacher and all they do is look to get you."

That's word for word. It's the type of statement that is hard to forget.

I remember thinking about how the guy could say that knowing that the Principal was new to the building and how we were a group of new people. Why taint us so early? I mean I have three Uncles who are/were building administrators and they proved pretty trustworthy my whole life. But, I filed it away and began my career with the island approach. That's the teaching method of closing your door, teaching your class, eating lunch with a friend or two, being around in case kids needed you, and going home.

The approach was successful with kids, but it did invite some trouble. I had a department chair who purposely put my classroom in the room that adjoined her office. She would sit by the door and write down things I would say. Then, she would quiz me about why I said them. It was combative in every way. I was 22 years old and so sure I had all the answers and here was the person in her last year giving me a hard time every day. Maybe the union chief was on to something.

My department chair's closest friend was the new assistant principal. That didn't bode well for me. The assistant principal would walk the halls, seemingly looking for me and all of the other teachers to mess up. She seemed to get happy when she caught me on a day that I failed to sign in at the main office. She came to my room right at the start of period one, unlocked the door, walked in like a combination of Cosmo Kramer and an army General about to do an inspection and interrupted me mid-sentence as I was teaching.

"Mr. Armida. You are in dereliction of your professional responsibilities. You didn't sign in!"

She sat there with the sign in sheet in her right hand, held high. It looked like a movie courtroom drama where the lawyer is holding the key piece of evidence. She said a bunch of other things, but I was trying not to curse at her in front of my eighth graders. She said for me to meet her in her office on my lunch to discuss this matter.

I gave her a flippant "ok" and continued teaching until she left. I'll admit that when she left, I stopped teaching and ran to a dictionary to look up what dereliction meant. I went into her office and she began to lecture. Then, I made a mistake; I yelled.

"You have no right to talk with me like this. I forgot to sign in, but that's because the list wasn't out when I got in. I was here with kids in my room, check that list. Or, is just more fun to try and write me up?"

That got me the first of many notes in my file. There were many more, from supposedly not being on hall duty on time to not proctoring a final exam properly. Year one certainly proved that head building rep correct.

But, a lot of it was my fault. That island approach is easy to slip into, but it gives off a certain vibe that you aren't interested in learning, listening to other professionals, being a part of a team, and being a part of something bigger than your four walls.

Yes, those two particular administrators were not the greatest of people, but if they were in my life now---and, to some degree, their personalities types are still there---I would've handled things much differently. It didn't take long for my approach to change.

The department chair retired and with that came the hiring of one of the most influential educators in my life. His first department meeting was an example lesson of how to get kids more involved in the writing process. When a department member asked him how he fits it all in, he gave an answer that I still use today. "What's more important, having a kid truly master writing

10

skills or that they read whatever number of books?" He concluded by saying that he would welcome any of us to his room.

I didn't take him up on the offer. But, it didn't take long for me to wind up in his classroom. After he observed me the first time, he met with me and gave me a litany of positives. He told me that I was a natural teacher and that kids responded to me. He then said, "they are doing the work for you and because of you. We have to get them to do the work because they want to."

That one sentence changed everything. Here was a guy who was clearly a master teacher and he went into administration to make the profession better. He got the principal to waive my lunch duty for a while so I could go watch him teach the writing process. I learned things that I still use to this day. And, I learned them from an administrator. He became a mentor and we began to talk about my issues with that particular assistant principal. I was surprised when he told me that I had a lot of the blame in these situations.

"Nobody comes into the profession wanting to be miserable or wanting to be the person who is always looking for trouble," he said.

He then asked me to look at myself and think about what I am projecting. My silence and mistrust projected a know-it-all vibe. It projected someone who didn't care about rules and procedures. It projected that I didn't want to get better. All of that hid the fact that I was pretty good in a classroom and really wanted to do well.

This wasn't just one conversation. This took months of talks. One day, he asked if I trusted him. Of course, I did. He was not only a mentor and my boss, but he was a friend. He said that I would have to let go of that old school mentality of not trusting administration and build relationships. I argued that the assistant principal relationship was too far gone, but he countered with the idea of showing respect, being honest, owning up to my mistakes, and making a fresh start.

He was far ahead of his time, some 20 years before Jimmy Casas, in his book Culturize, would write passionately about the idea of working collaboratively and building a culture of kid's first that administrators and teachers bought into. As Casas would say, someone is killing culture if they are working alone. In order to build culture, people must work together.

I did have that conversation and it did improve things, to the point where I didn't get notes in my folder. We still clashed, but we were able to talk. I'd be lying if I said we became friends; we didn't, but we were able to come to a common ground of me respecting her methods and her knowing that I wouldn't be perfect, but I was always there for the kids and was dependable.

That second year of teaching laid the groundwork of becoming the teacher I am today. My department chair's mentorship taught me that if we truly want to make a difference in schools and make them better for kids, we have to work as a team. There is no division where once you become an administrator, you lose all feelings for the classroom or forget what it is like to be a teacher.

Often, those are excuses we teachers make when our bosses tell us we have to do something different. Now, it is never going to be a perfect relationship because these are two very different roles. Administrators have to see the big picture while teachers can really focus on their four walls. Sometimes, the greater good doesn't match the needs of one individual. But, this is where trust has to be developed. Even if a principal or a superintendent makes a decision I don't agree with, I have to trust that they are making the best choice for the greatest number of kids given their circumstances.

How can I trust that?

Well, that's where building a real relationship comes into play. Like any relationship, it takes work to form trust between a teacher and an administrator. That doesn't mean you have to be friends with your administrators, but that's possible. I mean, you may even, one day, write a book with your assistant superintendent.

The first rule is to be willing and open. If you want to develop a good working relationship with your administrator, you have to be willing. Those big picture things that administrators see are very different from the world where we teachers live in. So, you may love teaching your particular grade level and may even be masterful at it. You may love the schedule you have, the team you are on, and even the duties you have, but you have to be willing to lead change. By being willing, you are showing that you trust the vision of your boss. You trust that they are making decisions that are best for kids. They may not be the same decisions you would make or in the same manner that you would make them, but you have to have that faith that this is what is best for kids.

Admittedly, this isn't always easy. About 10 years into my teaching career, I had found my groove as a 10th grade English Teacher. I had taught the level for five years and felt I had a good gig. I was comfortable, was creative, and was reaching kids by making the curriculum my own. My principal called a colleague who was a social studies teacher and me into his office and pitched us his idea. He identified that a high number of ninth grade students were failing English and Social Studies. Rather than have them repeat, he wanted us to create an alternative program for this group.

And, by the way, we would be teaching it.

Inside, I was a little upset.

Change is always hard. I had just gotten through some pretty rough years and had enjoyed the relative calm. Outwardly, I said yes. I trusted that this would be great for kids. My colleague and I created a great humanities-based program with alternative, grade level work, character education, and even a counseling component. It was a great, productive year. And, more importantly, it got those kids back on track. Most of them doubled up on courses and were able to graduate on time.

Because I was open and willing, my principal began to trust me. We--the principal, my social studies colleague, and an assistant principal--completely redesigned our 9th grade summer school program for that summer. I was thinking that I would return to my 10th grade gig, but my principal had other ideas.

"Listen, you did a great job with the program, but I'm moving you out of it."

"Ok, going back to 10 Honors?"

"You're going to take over the ESL program."

I didn't respond. I stared at him, processing what he just said. So, he kept talking.

"Listen, the program is struggling. Their Regents scores aren't even close to the grades they are getting in class. I'm putting you in my greatest area of need."

"I don't speak Spanish. How will I do my thing with them?"

"You don't need to speak Spanish. Go teach them. I'm trusting you with this."

At first, I thought he was punishing me for some reason, but he said he was trusting me with this. And, if I look at it now, he really was trusting me. I didn't speak the language, never taught 11th grade, and had no idea about teaching ESL.

It turned out to be the best thing to ever happen to my career.

I spent the next five years with some of the hardest working, honest kids. We became one of the highest scoring groups in the school. But, honestly, I don't remember that when I think about them. I think about all of the experiences, the laughs, and all the things we learned together. None of that would've happened if I didn't trust my principal or if I hadn't been willing to change for the big picture that I couldn't see yet.

It is easy to get comfortable and to react negatively to a proposed change. But, the majority of administrators don't just sit in offices and make changes for the sake of change. Most changes are thoughtful and are in the best interest of kids in mind. If you can show you are willing, you will be exposed to some of the best things the education world has to offer. I have gotten teach every grade level and almost every type of English/Language Arts course. That experience has made me a better teacher because I see the development process, I can pull different methods for different age groups, and, most importantly, I can continue to reinvent myself in the classroom.

By showing that you are willing, it will build trust with the administrator. It will allow you to pitch your ideas and changes. Because I have shown that I am all in, I can walk into an administrator's office and give reasons why we need to revamp our curriculum or, as I did a couple of years ago, say that we need to rip up our curriculum and start from scratch. Because they have seen me perform in their initiatives, they understand my work ethic and trust my judgement. That allows me to do curriculum projects, pitch new courses for kids, argue for no mandated summer assignments. If I want administrators to trust my judgement in the classroom, I have to give them that same trust.

The second rule is a foundation of every relationship, honesty.

Sounds simple, right?

But, it sometimes goes against everyone's nature when it comes to dealing with your boss. After all, they could fire you or, at least, put notes in your file. For something as simple as a family event, teachers will fake being sick or come up with elaborate stories. New teachers fear the need to take a day for a doctor's appointment or for family reasons. I see teachers stressing about their own children being sick and not knowing what to do about care. Teachers will stress about missing their own children's school events because, well, they are in the same profession and work the same hours. In almost 99 percent of the cases, complete honesty will solve problems.

Honesty is the only way to go in any professional situation. I was presented with a situation that would cause me to have to ask for help. There was an important doctor's appointment on the same day that we were scheduled to grade the seventh and eighth grade ELA exam. This day has always been one of my "hot button" days as some teachers would call out sick or work so slow while grading and leave the rest of us to grade hundreds of papers. I always made a point to show up first, work fast and efficient, and be a part of the core team that did the lion's share of the work. I almost panicked when I found out just six days prior that the appointment with a nationally renowned doctor was the same day.

Complicating this issue was that I had no relationship with the Middle School's new principal. It was the first year of our district's transformation and the school had a new principal who had a reputation of being quite efficient and having high expectations. My middle school colleagues loved working for him, but they always harped on his high expectations. Here I was, having never met him, about to let him down. It was even more important because he took over the organization of the grading, making the plan that seemed much more streamlined, professional, and efficient. Now, I was going to bail on him and the team just days before.

Some colleagues said to just call out that day and say it was an emergency. Even one high school administrator told me the same. But, I just couldn't do that. If I was to ever work with the new principal, Dr. Kris Felicello--yes, The Admin--in the future, this would be bad. More importantly, I needed to show that I respected him and the work he put into all of this. So, I emailed him that night. I wish I had a copy of that email because I remember taking a long time to write it. I wrote every detail, how I felt about being responsible with grading, and how this was the only option. I even offered to come in early to set up or come back late in the day to help finish. I closed with a sincere apology and the offer of bringing in doctor notes and whatever else he needed. I clicked send.

Four minutes later, he responded. He wrote:

> Gary,
>
> Don't worry about the grading. Thank you for reaching out and letting me know ahead of time. I hope everything goes well.
>
> Kris

With that, I was able to have a clear conscious at work. I met Kris a month later and thanked him for understanding. He said that he appreciated that I reached out as soon as I found out. If I wasn't honest with him that day, who knows what perception he would've held. Would he have chosen me to be the new English Department Coordinator, help lead initiatives in our district, or even work on our website? Although he was an unknown administrator to me, I decided to be honest rather than deceive or hide behind the false sick day.

A major component of honest is owning things, especially mistakes. Looking back at my (non) relationship with that assistant principal from my early years,

I realize there were moments when I should've owned up to my mistakes. She was correct to write me up for improper proctoring. I wasn't following the rules; I was reading a newspaper. There was no excuse. But, rather than own it, I yelled and I fought, which further drove a wedge between us. It also put the principal in a rough spot. He liked me, but I was also battling with one of his assistants. All I needed to do was say, "you're right. I was wrong and I'll never do it again." Instead, I fought and even let the union file a grievance.

Owning mistakes builds that trust.

In many ways, I am the typical English Teacher. I see the big idea, I get lost in the lofty points and absolutely loathe the minutia. This extends into things like paperwork, progress reports, and even report cards. I get they are important, but I just see the boring details that gets in the way of the cool stuff.

Well, around the time I was teaching ESL, we moved to another grading system. Now, I am pretty good with tech so I tend to not read the directions thoroughly. So, when it came time to report cards, I put final grades in the wrong column. All 132 students had the wrong grade. The calculations, their transcripts, everything was messed up.

I got the dreaded phone call to come to see our Assistant Principal of Guidance. She wasn't the type that you wanted to get a phone call from. Imagine Dwight Schrute and Angela Martin from the television show The Office had a baby girl and she grew up to be an assistant principal. That's who I was reporting to. It wasn't going to be pretty. After all, this was a person who, when she observed me, said "at minute 14, you said...why?" She's also the person who emails and calls teachers to remind them that they are late in entering progress reports, even when there is still a couple of hours left to the deadline.

So, this was a big mistake. I thought about blaming the new system. After all, I was the tech savvy guy and she was someone who preferred the mimeograph. I could probably make a good argument. The younger me would've. But, then I thought of the conversation with my former department chair.

Nobody comes to work in a school to make it worse, at least on purpose.

She had a job to do, which was to get report cards out to parents who were waiting on them. Because I was careless, I derailed that.

So, I went into her office and said, "before you say anything, I want to apologize. I messed up. I'll stay and do whatever needs to be done to fix them, including handwriting them if need be. And, whatever action has to come against me, I understand. No excuses."

To my surprise, she didn't yell. She patted me on the shoulder and said, "buddy, you messed up. Here's what you need to do..."

There was no yelling or notes in the file. Because I owned up and was willing to accept any consequence, we simply fixed it. Had I gone in with a lie, that would've gone differently.

Yes, owning up to a big mistake at work is scary. We all have that fear of getting fired or getting yelled at by our bosses. But, owning up and being honest creates trust. Your bosses know that you are reliable and someone with integrity.

Because of my honesty, administrators are honest with me. People in all businesses, even the education business, like to play this Game of Thrones type game where they maneuver to get what they want. They do this to try to avoid hearing the word no, but in honest relationships, that will happen. Although I have positive relationships with my administrators, they will tell me no when I ask for things from time to time. Even "The Admin" will say no to some of my requests. Because of our relationship, they will tell me why, rather than dismiss me. This is because we have developed trust and can be completely honest. Then, we can work together for a creative solution.

And, that is another rule to remember: always come with solutions. One of the things that tears at teacher-admin relationship is when the teacher comes expecting the administrator to solve the problem. Obviously, there are times when you are lost and need guidance. But, those situations cannot be the norm. Instead, a teacher can identify a problem and bring it to the attention of the administrator. The good administrator will definitely listen, especially if there is a relationship built on honesty, ownership, and a willingness to adapt.

All of this comes down to one thing: respect. Bottom line, administrators are our bosses. As teachers, we run our classrooms and it does give a little bit of a boss feel. That creates this feeling of "no administrator can tell me what to do in the classroom". But, one of the best things about the education industry is that fact that it truly can be a team. By being willing to be part of a team, by being honest, by owning up to mistakes, and by always bringing solutions, the teacher-admin team can be powerful.

Of course, there will be naysayers who believe that teachers should be on one side, united against the administration. You will get the looks or even have some gossip about how you are one of the administrator's lackeys.

It's all noise.

If you are someone who is there to make schools a better place for kids, there is no choice. You must develop into a team with your administrators. You must be willing and open to working within their vision. You must be honest. You must own up to mistakes. You must always come with potential solutions to problems, not just complain. All of this creates trust. That trust and bond are powerful. It can transform schools. It can create a culture where students, learning, and the process are valued.

None of this happens without developing trust.

Trust Takeaways for Admins

→ Treat your staff the way you want them to treat their students.

→ Spend more time on relationships and less time on rules, when people know you care about them they do not need rules they will just do what's right.

→ Admit your mistakes, be honest, nothing destroys trust like a lie.

→ Sometimes you need to put yourself on the line to protect your team.

→ Put your teachers in a position to be successful, we all have strengths and weaknesses good leaders find ways to accentuate the strengths and hide the weaknesses.

→ Forgive, teaching is a mentally exhausting job even the best teachers will make mistakes.

→ Let your staff know what drives you and your decisions- and it should be about the kids!

→ Take the time to get to know people, it is more important than checking lesson plan books and completing paperwork.

→ Inspire your staff by sharing what is possible but always remember to keep it simple. Small steps in the right direction is progress!

Trust Takeaways for Teachers

→ Administrators often have to make decisions based on the big picture, not just our classrooms. That does not mean they don't care about kids.

→ Change in education is scary, but usually leads to some of the lessons you will give and receive during your career.

→ Showing that you are willing to change and take on new challenges that will benefit kids develops a trust that will open many doors for you as an educator.

→ Owning your mistakes does not make you weak; it develops trust with administrators and leads to honest conversations.

→ Just because an administrator says no to your request or idea doesn't mean they don't value you.

→ Always come with solutions when meeting with an administrator over a potential or perceived problem. If you don't, you are really just complaining.

→ Be honest about what is going on in your life. Most administrators will do whatever they can to help you.

→ Even the most difficult administrator doesn't come to work just to make life difficult. It is up to us to develop a relationship with them so we can do what's best for kids.

VOICES FROM THE FIELD...

Amaris Scalia, Assistant Principal, Haverstraw Elementary School

If you were to ask me what I think the most important aspect of working in a school is, I would say, without hesitation, relationships. In education, we are in the business of people and to work productively with people, we need to build positive relationships. Building relationships must be every educator's focus regardless of their role. Positive relationships create a positive school culture which is conducive to increased student engagement and achievement.

Each day I am intentional in building relationships with students, families, staff and colleagues. Although the dynamics of relationships in a school may vary, they all can be built with some simple actions.

- **Smile:** Wearing a smile shows others that you care and that you enjoy your school. It sends a positive message and elevates moods. Smiling makes it inviting to students, staff and visitors. Besides, smiling is contagious!
- **Communicate:** Get to know the people around you. Engage in conversations. Ask questions about their lives outside of school including their hobbies, interests and families. Follow up after important events, whether it's a celebration or the passing of a loved one. Show them that you care.
- **Listen:** Listen more and talk less. There will be many times when you are approached by someone, whether it's a scheduled appointment or an unannounced visit. Start by asking how you can help and then just listen. Let them have the time to express themselves. Simply listen to understand rather than listen to respond.
- **Be Kind:** Kindness goes a long way. Students, staff members and families should be treated with kindness at all times. Kindness demonstrates concern and consideration for others. It has a positive effect on the social emotional well-being of others. Kindness communicates that you care.

Relationships are not hard to build; however, conscious effort is necessary. Just like a garden, relationships will not grow on their own, they need care and attention. When you do just that, they will blossom and flourish.

2

Parent Involvement

*"Alone we can do so little. Together we can
do so much." ~ Helen Keller*

While a teacher and admin team are a great start to make schools a better place for kids, it is just that---a good start. Schools are more than just about the people who work there. They are bigger than that, a fact that often eludes even the most well-intentioned educators.

All schools serve their communities.

Great schools are their communities.

That community starts with the belief that parents are an integral and irreplaceable part of our team. They are entrusting us, educators, with their children. If we truly want to make schools better for kids, having parents be a welcomed, important part of the team is a vital step.

There are times when it may seem like we are on opposite sides. When it comes

23

to their kids, parents will, rightfully, do anything. Sometimes, grades, behavior incidents, questions about practices, or something that upsets a child may seemingly put the educator and parent on opposite sides. That's not the case and we must never let that be the case. It is in those moments where we, the educators, must remember that parents are a part of our team. And, we must do our very best to demonstrate that to them every time, even in the most difficult situations.

The Admin

As a school community, we need to do everything we can to make parents feel welcome, to have them see the "us" as a "we".

Educators get the best outcomes for students when the school is seen as the hub for the community, when parents not only feel comfortable entering the school, but want to be there.

It often starts as soon as parents walk into the door of our schools.

How do you feel when you walk into a new place? A place that you are unfamiliar with.

For me, I get a little uneasy, feel a bit timid, maybe a bit anxious that I will say or do something that I am not supposed to do. Now imagine a parent who walks into your school, who may not have had the best experience with school when they were a child.

It is important to help guests feel at home, consider greeting them with a smile and asking them how we can serve them.

I see it as the job of the leader to work with staff to do everything they can do to ensure the school is a comfortable environment. When leaders model how they expect visitors to be treated and take the time to explicitly describe what each employee's role is this vital task everyone benefits.

If the office staff does not look up when someone walks in, if the phones are not answered properly, if there is an eye roll for the disruption of the task at hand, the responsibility to correct this lies with the leader. Todd Whitaker once told me that when your school staff does not meet your expectations, they are either uninformed or insubordinate.

Too often in the past I have assumed the latter and not taken the time to be specific with my expectations. I have found that most times when I am courageous enough to clearly explain what I expect and teach "the why" behind those expectations, most employees are happy to do the right thing.

Most educators emphasize the importance of the home school connection, yet unintentionally we put barriers up, especially for parents who are already uncomfortable in our space. We rarely dedicate our time to discuss what we can do to make parents want to come to our school. I have found that time spent discussing, strategizing ways that we can build bridges with parents is a great use of a faculty meeting.

Educators who think about ways to make entering their school the best possible experience for parents can improve the home to school connection. Establishing protocols that protect the safety of students are efficient, but it is also important to consider how these protocols affect parents. Some ideas that I have implemented or observed other schools that have been great ways to build relationships with parents:

It's the Little Things

Good News Cards

For a minimal cost, you can have postcards printed with the school logo or picture of the building on the front, with "Good News From..." scrolled across the card. I used to send these cards home to students and encourage staff to do the same. My wife took this idea one step further. She uses the first five minutes of her monthly faculty meetings to have teachers fill out two or three good news cards. She has mailing labels preprinted for each teacher based on their class list. Her strategy gives teachers the time, makes it convenient, and ensures that each child gets at least one good news card for the year.

THE **TEACHER** & THE **ADMIN**

Pictures

As a young Athletic Director, I heard a veteran present on branding. Of course, it wasn't called branding back then, but that is exactly what he was doing. Each time he went to an athletic contest he would take a few pictures, have them printed out, and mail them home to parents. He would check off the student/athlete's name off the team roster each time he sent home a picture. I implemented this strategy, and it was so successful for me that I continued doing it when I was named principal. Now, instead of pictures home for just athletic contests, I mailed students' pictures home for concerts, Halloween costumes, Student of the Month awards, and other school highlights.

As a parent, I understand the joy in seeing my child's happiness or success away from the nest. There is something special about a printed picture that can be hung on the fridge for years to come. But, if that is cost prohibitive, a digital picture emailed or sent through Class Dojo can have the same effect.

Parents Center

As principal of Fieldstone Middle School, I always wanted to create a Parents Welcome Center. My vision was a space for parents to have a cup of coffee, make a phone call, or just gather their thoughts as they wait to pick up their child, a conference with a teacher, or a CSE meeting.

Surveys

With tools like SurveyMonkey and Google Forms, creating surveys and analyzing results has never been more convenient. It is always a good idea to offer the school community a venue to offer their thoughts, suggestions, and provide their feedback. Setting up Chromebooks during school events is a great way to increase participation in surveys. Completing a survey while waiting for a meeting with a teacher is a great way to utilize time.

Communication

Communication is not just about a newsletter, progress report, email, social media, phone calls, report cards, tech tools like remind.com, and face to face communication. It is about all of those strategies and more.

The world has become such a busy place; communication has changed. If there is an issue in school, parents sometimes know before the administration.

How do we deal with this? How do we deal with it when parents show up unannounced or call demanding a resolution immediately?

There is no easy answer, but remembering it is not personal is the first step, showing respect is a second. You do not have to drop everything for an irate parent, but taking a minute to greet them and schedule a time to meet goes a long way. I have also found having a secretary call back a parent and explaining that you got their message and plan to call them back when your meeting is finished can help to ease the parent's anxiety and make the situation better in the long run. A quick call letting a parent know that there was an issue involving their child, that their child is safe, that you are investigating the situation, and that you will get back to them as soon as you have more information is a strategy that I may not have used before the smartphone era, but is one that is beneficial in our instant information world. There is no one magic bullet for parent communication; it is about various strategies, and always being cognizant of how a parent may be feeling.

School Events
If it is parent-teacher conferences, meet the teacher night, or a special event, it is important to remember that the devil is in the details. Be sure to advertise your event on your website, with students, on flyers, and with robocalls or emails. When guests are arriving at the school, have greeters at the door letting them know where to go and what to expect. Maps, agendas for the event, and other school literature can make a world of difference. Having Honor Society, or other student volunteers available in the hallways to serve as tour guides or to answer questions is a great strategy to not only help guests, but to offer students the opportunity to give back.

When you build relationships with parents, when you emphasize the importance of treating parents as clients, when you work with staff to determine the best ways to partner with parents, it makes a school more welcoming and only helps when you have a difficult situation or a conflict with a difficult parent.

I often think back to one of the most difficult parents I had as an educator. I was a middle school principal in a small district in upstate New York. One of my sixth graders, one of the most challenging students I have ever worked with, was dealing with a lot of pain and sorrow that was easy to detect just by looking into his eyes. That pain manifested in some bizarre behaviors that forced me to invoke consequences.

One particular infraction had the student in my office for most of the day as I investigated what was referred to as "the dead bird incident". Bill had wrapped a present and put it on the classmate's desk. The present included a card that read, "Susan, I love you. Will you be my girlfriend?"

When the girl opened the box, she found a dead bird with a note that said, "Psych, I'm actually going to kill you."

Obviously, this girl was distraught and our school became consumed with finding the culprit. We had a pretty good idea that it was Bill based on the handwriting, the fact it was next to his desk, and that he was the only student who had access to the room without a teacher present.

After questioning him a few times, he finally owned up to his mistake. This led to a multi-day suspension and superintendent hearing. His father couldn't believe how unreasonable we were being. He felt what his son had done wasn't a big deal. He saw the dead bird as a practical joke, one similar to putting water above a room door and soaking the occupants when it was opened.

I didn't see it this way and explained my thoughts to dad. We went back-and-forth for about an hour or so. It was 6 o'clock and the office was empty except for a secretary who was working late. I was trying to be calm, trying to reason with him, but I lost my cool when he said he no longer gave me permission to speak to his son.

I explained that it was "my school" and I had the right and the responsibility to question students whenever I saw fit.

My statement, although legally correct, was probably not the best approach with an already angry parent. He took exception to the "my school" statement and it triggered him to slam his hands on my desk and come at me, pointing his finger in my face. I stood my ground, locked eyes with him, and inched a bit closer keeping my hands on my side, but clearly telling him I wasn't afraid of his nonsense. The secretary heard the commotion and with a quiver in her voice asked, "everything OK?" I told her to call the police, which prompted Dad to leave after a few more profanity-laced comments.

Three months later, I found myself in court testifying against one of my student's parents. I remember telling that story and, at the time, I was proud I stood up to him. I showed him!

Now, I realize how poorly I handled that situation. I took dad's anger, his unreasonableness, his aggression, personally.

What did my "pound of flesh" accomplish? What did I "show him?"

My student was already in pain, was already suffering, and someone who was supposed to be there for him made the situation worse.

I've often reflected on that day, thinking about how I could have done better.

Parents are, at times, unreasonable because they care more about their child than anything else in this world. When you have so much love for someone, you don't always see straight. The best leaders do not take poor behavior personally. Are there some parents that are just jerks? Absolutely, but in those cases, it is even more important to remember it is about the student. If their dad is acting inappropriately with the principal of the school, can you imagine how they treat their child at home?

The best leaders never take it personally even when they are dealing with the most difficult parents.

The best leaders never "big time" parents. They do not try to prove how smart they are; they do not point out all the ways the parent is wrong. They don't craft that witty email that proves just how right they are. I always try to keep this in mind, and although I have gotten better since "the bird incident" I still slip and fall into old habits sometimes. It is not easy to swallow your pride and show respect for parents who may not deserve it.

I try to coach the principals I serve so they do not make the same mistakes I did. I explain that they may be right; they may craft a great email, but, at the end of the day, they may feel a bit better, but they are not doing what is in the best interest of their school or their students.

Remember what it feels like to be in a situation where you feel you have no control. Put pride aside and listen, let them say their peace, be respectful. Be calm and, most of all, be kind.

Let parents know that we want to help their children just as much as they do. Sometimes it means eating a little crow; sometimes it means apologizing, even if we don't want to or even if they don't deserve it. We do because ultimately, it's better for our students. We apologize not because we were wrong, but because we want to repair the relationship.

This doesn't mean you are weak. It doesn't mean that you let parents dictate how you run your school.

I feel it is essential to make a well-informed decision and stick by that decision regardless of how loud or aggressive a parent may get.

When I say respect parents, I do not mean let them call the shots. In fact, I think it is dangerous to change a decision just because of a squeaky wheel parent. This practice can lead to inequity that puts students whose parents are appropriate or absent at a disadvantage.

Some strategies to help with difficult parent conversations

- Find something you have in common.
- Never use sarcasm.
- Be honest and real.
- Ask them for suggestions on how you can work together for their child.
- Call them or set up a face to face rather than responding to a nasty email.
- Use a common language, avoid using "edulingo".
- End a heated conversation and promise to revisit it after they have had a chance to cool down.
- Stay calm, keep your voice low.

- Avoid bringing up past indiscretions; keep bringing them back to the issue at hand .

When they bring up other issues or claims of what is wrong with your school tell them you would be happy to investigate, but remind them of the issue at hand.

Parents often claim things were handled differently for other children. Do not discuss other students and what their consequences may or may not have been.

One of the most challenging situations an administrator will come across is when a parent is upset with something that one of your staff members did and that they, the parents, are correct. You have to support your teacher; you have to have their back, it is a non-negotiable. Yet, we also serve parents and always have to put kids first.

It is our job to bring parents and teachers together, doing our best to repair a relationship that may be damaged. The first strategy I have found to often be the most successful is to get out of the way. Nine times out of ten when you direct a parent to discuss their concerns directly with the teacher, they can come up with a solution.

It is that one out of ten that keeps us up at night. I have found that in most situations you need to do some work before facilitating a meeting or phone call.

Get the information from the parent's perspective; get the information from the teacher's perspective. Try to objectively look at what you have discovered.

Remember that it is not who is right and who is wrong, but to come to an outcome that is in the student's best interest. Here are a few strategies that can be helpful in achieving that goal:

- Talk to your teacher before the parent meeting. If you think the teacher is wrong, be honest and see if they have a suggestion for making it right.
- Never embarrass your teacher in front of the parent and visa versa.
- Find out what it is the parent is looking for to resolve the situation.
- You do not have to make a difficult decision on the spot. Let both the

teacher and the parent know that you appreciate the information they have provided and you will get back to them with your decision.

- Coach your teacher prior to the meeting, let them know what to expect, how the parent may react, and what any underlying issues may be.
- Establish the goal of the meeting you are facilitating. "We are meeting today because Mrs. Smith is upset because Mrs. Jones took away Stephan's recess. We are going to try to work together to do what is in Stephan's best interest."
- Establish expectations for the meeting. No voices raised, no personal attacks or insults, no cursing.
- Stay on track; redirect when the parent or teacher brings up a past grievance.
- Never, ever allow a parent to be inappropriate with your teachers. If they are unable to follow your expectations, end the meeting and promise to discuss at a later date when emotions are less raw. As a leader, I am able to take it when a parent gets inappropriate with me, but I will never let a parent go after one of my teachers or administrators.

The Teacher

To be honest, I never fully understood the importance of parental involvement during the first half of my career. I had always thought that my job was to teach kids. I never once blamed parents for anything other than those extreme cases of neglect or abuse. But, if a kid wasn't engaged or wasn't doing the work, I didn't blame "these parents today" or anything. It's my job to motivate, to connect, and to get a kid to go "all in".

I still truly believe all of that. I never blame a parent for something that is or isn't happening in my classroom. But, I have looked at the role of a parent in the education process quite differently since September of 2012.

The significance of September 2012?

It's simple really. That was the year my daughter entered Kindergarten, the first time she would be in "real" school for a full day. I remember the feeling I had on that first day. I spent the day wondering what she was doing, if she was scared, if she was making friends, and how she was going to do. I knew she was smart, but I realized that I had more than a little bias in that belief. Suddenly, the doubt of whether or not I performed my duties as a parent also crept in. Would she be polite? Would we get called into the Principal's office because she said something inappropriate? Did the manners we stressed at home happen when we weren't there looming over her? Fortunately, I am blessed to have a great daughter so all of those things came out to be positive as she navigated her way through her school career thus far.

But, all of that gave me a new perspective on the idea of parental involvement. While I would always engage with parents, speak with them at length at conferences, and answer any questions they may have, I didn't put a whole lot of thought into how I can make them feel a part of the team and how I could let them know that I truly value the trust they are putting in me. After all, they are trusting me to teach their children. That's a heavy responsibility that should never be taken lightly.

That sentiment really goes for any level. Sure, it is more palpable and much more involved with parents of elementary students. But, parents of Middle School and High School students still have those feelings about how their child is doing. I use the word "child" purposely. No matter how old, a parent will always view their offspring as their child. Sometimes, we at the secondary level can forget that as we foster the ideals of independence. Yes, it is our job to develop all of those skills so that students can enter adulthood well prepared, but I have learned that it is also our job as educators to offer opportunities for parents to be involved and be a part of the educational team. After all, they are trusting us to teach their kids. We do work for them.

The first step---and really the only thing we can do---is to invite parents to have a relationship with us on equal footing. We must be secure enough in our skills as an educator to welcome parents into the conversations. In truth, elementary teachers do this really well. They communicate with parents on almost a daily basis whether it is through communication logs, the homework agenda, multiple parent-teacher conferences, emails, or the quick conversations at pickup time. Because of the nature of the age group, it is almost as if it is expected. It should be expected.

We at the secondary level must take our cue from our colleagues at the elementary level. There is no excuse for a lack of communication with a parent. There is no excuse for a parent to not know who their child has for a teacher. If the parent doesn't know, it is more than likely because we did not reach out enough to create that communication.

Back to the first step, we have to invite the parents to have a relationship with us. Even as a high school teacher, I send a welcome letter home on the first day and post it on my parent website. The letter doesn't mention anything about supplies or curriculum. I introduce myself, my philosophy of education, and give out all the ways to contact me. The biggest part of the letter is my explicit explanation that I, indeed, work for them and value the trust they are giving me. I also invite them to reach out if they have ideas, concerns, or thoughts about what's going on in the room.

A letter, however, is not enough. It is a good first step. On the secondary level, the first weeks of school usually include a night time "Meet the Teacher Night". This night is usually an opportunity for parents to walk their child's schedule and get a quick talk from each teacher, usually less than 10 minutes. Many teachers look at this night as a waste of time. Spend a few minutes in a teacher's lounge or a department office and you will inevitably get the line, "this is a terrible night, nothing gets accomplished."

I've always loved these nights, even when I didn't know the significance of them. Early in my career, I looked at is as a way to make a good first impression. I reasoned that if they were confident that I knew what I was doing and that I looked professional, I wouldn't have issues. That reasoning is quite embarrassing now, but the idea of making a good first impression is the right idea and one of the important parts of the night. As a parent, you want to see that your child is with a good, prepared teacher. While my early days had the wrong reasons, I was at least showing that I was prepared and cared enough to have a presentation.

But, again, having my daughter in school cleared this process up for me. Each year, those "Meet the Teacher Nights" would impress me as her kindergarten, second, and third grade teachers really showed me that they knew their curriculum, but, more importantly, cared about each child in the class. This was even more crystallized during my daughter's fourth grade year.

Her teacher began her talk with us by talking about the class and its personality. She talked about them as human beings and how they were so much fun in the first weeks. She then began to talk about how much she loved teaching, loved teaching fourth grade, and that she couldn't wait to teach this one particular social studies unit. She eventually hit on all of the curriculum, but she also made a point to have a quick chat with each parent, saying something she knew about the child. I left that night knowing that my daughter had the best teacher. And, more importantly, I felt that she already knew my daughter and cared. She would prove that over and over again throughout the year. But, that first "Meet the Teacher Night" gave me true insight into the woman who would be spending the next 10 months with my daughter. It was all I really wanted.

There is zero reason why this can't happen on the secondary level. Over the years, I have become more open on these nights. Two years ago, my purpose for the night, as well as parent-teacher conferences, became clear. I was in our English Office when one of the teachers opined that the Meet the Teacher Night was a waste and was looking for me to agree. I found myself saying the opposite.

"I love these nights. We are selling hope to parents."

Yes, it is corny and, yes, I got some eye rolls, but it was the truth. One colleague asked what I meant.

"Parents want to know that their kids have a teacher who is all in. They want to know that there is someone in the room who they can trust, talk to, and who will teach their kids. We are selling them the hope that their kid will be ok both in and out of the classroom."

Yes, I said those words. And, yes, I did get more eye rolls. I got even more eye rolls when I put that on our department agenda a couple of months later before parent-teacher conferences.

We have to create the relationship so parents feel like they can reach out with concerns about their child, reach out about something that is confusing them, or reach out for advice about what to do with their child, both the good and the not so good. The opening letter is a formality. The Meet the Teacher Night is when the real relationship can begin.

Some schools may give their teachers a script on what to say. Unions will likely give a list of what to say and what not to say. All of that is fine, but you only have one chance to make that impression and, more importantly, create a productive relationship for the betterment of kids.

My past few Meet the Teacher Nights have generally run the same way. First, I start by introducing me and how I feel about teaching. Two years ago, for the first time, I said, "I love my job." I don't know why it took me 20 years to say that to a group of parents, but I finally did. I remember some of the looks of surprise on high school parents. It did set a tone of welcome and they knew from that statement that I actually wanted to be there. After that, I immediately talk about the personality of the class and the first impression I have. It is always positive. It isn't a stock line.

Two years ago, much like every year, I had three distinct class personalities. My period two class was quite quiet, but hardworking and had a great sense of humor. My period three class was the loudest, funniest, most caring class I've ever taught. And, my fourth period, had a unique mix of deep thinkers, jokers, and were all hard workers. While I didn't know all of that after four days of class, I was able to tell each group of parents something about the makeup of the class. When I do that, parents are smiling, picturing their child. I'll also have information because I don't focus on content during the first week. We are getting to know each other, writing some personal or creative pieces, and doing a lot of talking.

After discussing the personality of the class, I will show parents a quick overview of the course for about 30 seconds and then give my contact information. While they got it the first day, parents can be seen writing it down or putting in their phone. While they are doing this, I will tell them that I want them to contact me. I want to hear from them, both good and not so good. I leave them with two things: "I work for you" and "I want this class to be your child's favorite class and that can only happen with us working together." And, I will leave the last couple of minutes for questions.

That first night is important, but then the real relationship building actually starts. When a parent reaches out, you must act. It isn't just your job, it is your obligation to the parent. No matter how silly it may seem or no matter how right you may feel, you must deal in more than a professional manner. You must deal with them as a partner. Sure, some parents may have unreasonable requests, but most of those disappear if there is a solid relationship where the parent feels informed.

One way to develop this sort of trust is a simple email newsletter. Again, elementary teachers are excellent at this, but the secondary level has largely cast this aside with the idea of "I have a class page, it's on them to look".

No, we must cultivate the relationship.

I do have a parent email newsletter that I send out from time to time. Generally, I will give some details about what we are working on, a quick story about the class, and where we are heading. Sometimes, I will even attach an interesting article. It is a simple way---that isn't time-consuming---to making a parent feel included and part of the process. It opens up the lines because they can feel comfortable in approaching me.

Then, the relationship is strengthened during parent-teacher conferences. For new teachers and even veteran teachers, parent-teacher conferences can be scary. Most of that fear comes from two things: a lack of confidence and a lack of professional development. The industry pays lip service to the importance of the home-school connection, but little is done with new teachers—even veteran teachers—to help build relationships with parents. Because of the lack of training and development, the unconfident Teacher creates, at worst, an adversarial relationship. At best, fear creates a relationship that doesn't go beyond the numbers and curriculum of the class. Neither scenario is good for kids.

It took me years to learn how to conduct myself during conferences. Like most new Teachers, I was nervous when it came to Parent-Teacher Conferences. I was much younger than the people in the room and, truthfully, insecure about what I was doing with their kids during the day. So, my first few conferences, I had a line of parents waiting down the hallway. We just talked. I blabbed on about what we were doing in the class and the parents would ask questions about why we weren't doing spelling as they did in school and everything in between. It was fine insofar that I didn't have any real issues, but my line of waiting parents was always a good source of jokes by the veteran teachers.

As I was talking with Parents, the veteran Teachers would poke their heads in the room and say, "You have a long line out there. What are you giving away?"

I'm not sure if that was meant to be funny or if it was meant as a way of telling me to move things along, but it was embarrassing to be called out like that in front of Parents; it only led to more insecurity. After the last set of conferences of my third year of teaching, a veteran Social Studies Teacher pulled me aside. He was a nice enough guy, even if he always shook his head in disbelief at the new guy down the hall. He had some advice since he was retiring.

"Listen, kid, you have to stop talking so (expletive) long with the parents. They don't want to (expletive) hear anything other than the grade their kid is getting. You think they want to be here all (expletive) night? Give them the grade, tell them what their kid needs to improve and move on."

I behaved the same way I always did when he gave advice. I smiled and nodded. But, the next year, I kept the talking part in mind.

I ran "efficient" conferences. Parents came in and told me who they were. I started with the grade their son or daughter was getting and then talked about where we were going in the curriculum.
In and out in under two minutes. Parents were fine, but there was no real relationship. It became more about when things went wrong, rather than being together in all phases of education.

That went well for a few years until the embarrassing moment. A parent of one of my high achieving students came in to meet with me just after the first quarter. I had the typical formula.

"He is getting a 94 for the quarter, which is one of the better grades in the class considering he is transitioning from Middle School. 9th grade is a big jump. Next, we'll be reading…"

The parent cut me off.

"Why only a 94? He always got 97's in English."

I sat there in disbelief that we were talking about three points. But, the real problem was that I didn't have an answer. Why a 94 instead of a 97? What was the difference? How did I arrive at that number? I tried to deflect and talk about how a 94 is a great grade, but he wasn't having it.

Honestly, I couldn't explain it so I got defensive.

I flipped my grade book around and said, "Here. Write in whatever grade that will make you happy. If it is about a number, don't worry. 94, 97, there's no difference to me."

The Parent didn't write the number; he actually got a bit nervous trying to explain why he was questioning it. It was awkward, but we finished up the conference somewhat amicably. The next day, I told the story in the English office. People were congratulating me for "taking a stand." I took the adulation, but something didn't feel right, even years after.

Here's what didn't feel right: I didn't tell that parent one thing about his child. I didn't tell him what I could do to improve his child's already excellent performance in class. All I did was communicate that I was "the expert", he shouldn't question "the expert", and he should leave it "to the expert". It was a terrible message that came from an insecurity and a myopic perspective of what it meant to be "The Teacher."

I'd love to say that I immediately changed. While I always chatted with parents and was always about doing what was best for students, the actual communication of that was lacking. Parents liked me because their kids were happy. That was my connection with them. But, there should've been a whole lot more.

And, I am reminded every year after. As a Parent, I don't really care about the grade. I want to know that her teacher knows her as a person. I want to know that her Teacher knows her strengths and the things she needs to improve. I want to know that her Teacher has a plan. I want to know that she cares.

I want her to sell me some hope.

As corny as that sounds, that is a Teacher's primary job with both students and Parents. Each day, we have to teach kids those skills we believe are necessary for success. And, we have to offer them the hope that it will all pay off. And, we have to give Parents that same hope. All Parents want their kids to succeed. It is our job to keep that hope ignited within them, even with those kids who are challenging us.

So, now, once again, I have the longest lines for Parent-Teacher conferences. This time, it is for the right reasons. Grades are given if a parent asks for them. Instead, I talk to them about what their child brings to my class. I talk about what their child contributes to the class as a person and how we are better for it. If there is a deficiency that needs to be addressed, it is addressed by offering the solution first. And, I will always conclude with a question for them. They know their kids better than anyone; why would I ignore their input?

Most of my conferences have the following format:

Start with Something About Their Child, The Person.
It sounds simple, but it is overlooked. If a parent knows that you actually care about their child, the relationship will be sound. As each parent walks in, I will start with a quick story about something their child did in class. It could be something they said or something they wrote. Really, it could be anything. The further away from academics, the better. I want to show that I know their child and that their child means a lot to our class.

For the parent of the "easy" child, this will bring another smile to their face.

They have a good kid and they know it. It is always nice to hear that they are doing well when not under their supervision.

For the parent of the "not so easy" child, this will be different. After I tell them that "they work really hard and always is asking me questions about how to do better" or "they make me laugh every day when they come in and say…", I am usually met with "Are you sure you are talking about my child?"

When I say that I am, there is a smile of a different kind. Maybe it was the first positive comment they heard all night. Maybe it was just nice to hear something about their child, not what their child was lacking. It definitely gives a flicker of hope and the security that their child isn't just a number or some random kid in a class.

Most importantly, it shows that their child has a chance in my class. It shows that I know them and want them to do well and that we can work together to help the child.

Emphasize the Victories

Far too often, conferences turn into the "what's missing" session. It'll focus on missing work or skills that are lacking. While all of that has its place, every student has victories. It is important for parents to hear those, even if their child isn't meeting with success in class. For me, I have a notepad full of notes that I make when reading their writing. This allows me to give specific examples of some of the progress they are making. This isn't a conversation about grades. It is about how they are progressing as writers, readers, and critical thinkers.

By emphasizing the victories and having specific notes on each student, you now have credibility with the parents. You are showing that you see progress. You are showing that you are monitoring specific skills. You are giving specific examples. Unlike my embarrassing conference years ago, I am able to give specific information from the class.

You are giving parents content, not just some meaningless number. Doing that allows for more difficult conversations.

Start with The Plan for Addressing Deficiencies

The difficult part of conferences is discussing deficiencies that must be addressed. Often, teachers will just state them. I've done that plenty of times.

> *"...he doesn't give enough evidence in his writing...she doesn't write in complete sentences...she isn't reading the book...he didn't turn in this essay..."*

All of those things are true and definitely need to be communicated. But, simply saying those things is really just complaining to the parent. And, truthfully, it is not the parents' job to correct. It's our job. It's also like going to a Doctor and them telling you that you have high blood pressure and then leaving. Well, great, I have a problem; how do I fix it?

Instead, start with the solution.

"I am going to sit with him during class and work on backing up his ideas with more evidence. That's something we will work on."

"We are going to sit together during class or after school if she wants and work on writing complete sentences."

"I am going to start a book discussion group so we can dive into our class reading a little more and have her read more closely."

"I refuse to give him a pass on this assignment. We are going to meet and have him do this essay. It's important and something he's worked on in class."

All of those communicate a problem, but show the parent that you, the teacher, actually care. You have a plan and will do everything to have their child be successful. You aren't complaining to them. You are telling them what you are going to do to fix something.

My daughter's fourth grade teacher did this so well. My daughter, thankfully, is good at school. She picks things up quickly; we are lucky. But, she did tend to rush through things, especially reading. That would cause her to lose some of the important details of a story. At the first conference, her teacher brought it up.

"I'm going to invite her to our book club after school and we will work on reading carefully and learning how to read in between the lines."

As a parent, it was refreshing to hear that my daughter's teacher knew her so well, knew that she had an issue, and had a plan to fix it. And, because of her plan, there was huge progress just months later. Her teacher gave me hope that it would be fixed. I left there with confidence in her teacher and, as always, so proud of my daughter.

Finish with A Question

I always ask parents the same type of question at the end of a conference: Do you have any advice for me?

They are raising that child. They are the experts. Why not tap into that? Most of the time, you will get some really valuable insight into a student, as both a person and learner. This not only gives you that insight, but it builds a team. While I don't expect any parent to teach any content or be on top of their child about classwork, I do want parents to know that we are on the same side and we both want the same thing. We want their child to be successful. The only way we can have that is by talking and working together.

A few years back, I asked a parent that question. Her son was doing well, but was really quiet in class. Some kids are naturally quiet and there is nothing wrong with that. But, when I asked the parent if she had any advice, she told me that her son really didn't like working in groups. This was great information as I do quite a bit of group work. So, a few days later, I had him come early to class. Because I had this information, I was able to talk to him about why we do group work and why I believe it was important. Then, I asked him what he thought and what I could do to make it a better experience.

That conversation led to a couple of things. First, it led to us having a better relationship because I sought out his input. Second, it led to coming up with class group work norms; we set formal expectations for each member and each session, something I never thought had to be done. But, once we did, he worked better and participated more. And, honestly, the class group work ran better. All of that was because I asked for advice.

Without communicating with parents, letting them know you care about their kids and not just the number you put on the report cards, and that you value the parent's input can create a special relationship with a parent. It involves them without placing blame. It involves them to be a vital part of the team that they already are. And, it allows us to be better equipped to help our students. Parent involvement is about teamwork. It is about a productive relationship that is powerful and that makes schools a better place for kids.

Parent Involvement Takeaways For Admins

→ Always show parents respect.

→ Take the time to work with staff to establish strategies to make parents feel comfortable in your school.

→ Remember the importance of the little things- Notes, pictures, good news cards and more.

→ Use a wide variety of tools to communicate with parents.

→ Never take it personally when a parent is unreasonable.

→ Sometimes you need to swallow your pride in the best interests of a child.

→ Always remain calm when parents are upset.

→ Do your best to mend fences between guardians and staff members.

→ Establish creative and fun family events to make parents feel welcome.

→ Always keep in mind what is best for the student.

→ Be willing to take the blame for your teachers.

Parent Involvement Takeaways For Teachers

→ Parents trust us with their kids every day. Acknowledge that responsibility.

→ Parents are a part of the team - they are not the enemy.

→ A welcome letter introducing yourself and your core beliefs is a good first step.

→ "Meet the Teacher Night" is an opportunity to "sell some hope" to parents so they know that their child is valued, cared for, and will receive excellent instruction.

→ Continue to open the door to your classroom. Create a newsletter, update your website. All parents access to know what is going on in the classroom.

→ A teacher-parent relationship is more than just about a grade. It is the teacher's duty to make it about more than a grade.

→ Parent-Teacher Conferences should be about the whole child.

→ Every parent wants what is best for their child. Remember that if there is an occasion where a parent seems unreasonable. What wouldn't you do for your child? Ask a parent for insight on their child.

VOICES FROM THE FIELD...
Anthony Zollo, Principal, Fieldstone Middle School

Parent communication is a phrase which evokes fear in educators. Regardless of the number of years one has been working in our profession, the thought of holding contentious conversations with parents keeps educators awake at night. It is this type of thinking, coupled with the advent and application of various modalities of communication that is fostering the disconnect between educators and parents.

Technologies such as email blasts, text messages, social media platforms, and student management systems that allow parents to access grades in live time, has further deepened the divide between educators and parents.

Often, we as educators have defaulted to sending emails or uploading information to the "parent portal" with the belief that it alleviates our obligation to communicate essential information about students' performance with parents directly.

Please don't misunderstand. I firmly believe each of the aforementioned technologies serves a purpose in education. If used appropriately these technologies could expedite and even improve communication with parents.

However, when these mechanisms act in lieu of direct contact with parents, the gap between the two parties becomes greater. Even something as simple as a phone call directly to a parent drastically improves the likelihood of a positive exchange. In fact, I encourage all educators, that whenever time allows or the situation demands, a personal meeting with a parent is the best way to deescalate a potentially troublesome situation. Many caring parents who are engaged deeply in their child's education believe they are, in fact, the ultimate advocate for their children.

Unfortunately, while this belief may come from the purest of intentions it could lead to a fundamental disconnect between parents and educators. As educators, we are charged with the responsibility of helping channel the desire parents have to support their children. In my experience, it is the face to face interactions that personalize this process and lead parents to the realization of our shared goal.

By communicating directly, frequently and candidly, free from judgement we can best win over the support of parents.

3

Giving Students A Voice

"Student is not a container you have to fill,
but a torch you have to light up."
~ Albert Einstein

The teacher, admin, and parent team come together for one purpose: to make schools better for kids. But, there is one more element that is often overlooked in that process. It is the students. When looking to see how we can make education meaningful, it is important to give students that voice. In our roles, that is addressed in multiple ways.

As an administrator, it is important to set an environment where teachers feel like they have the freedom to ask kids for input. There needs to be an environment of allowing teachers to listen to student feedback and adjust. And, it is important for administrators to listen to the students themselves. Far too often, administrators lose touch with the kids they so desperately want to help. Allowing all students access and genuinely listening to their concerns while developing their skills can be powerful when it comes from an administrator.

As a teacher, the job is clear. Teachers should do everything possible to develop student voice. Everything done in the classroom must help develop their own voice so that they can go out in the world, know that they have value, and know that they can make a great impact. With that, students must have the opportunity to not only develop those skills, but take an active role in the learning that goes on in the classroom. By allowing students to have a voice in their education, we are creating active thinkers, active problem solvers, and future leaders.

The Admin

I remember my first day as a school administrator very well. It was August first and I was starting a new position as Athletic Director and Assistant Principal in a small school district in New York State. The building I walked into could have been straight out of a Norman Rockwell painting. The street the school sat on even had a Rockwellesque name...Maple Avenue. I walked in not knowing what being an administrator entailed, not knowing if I was cut out to be an administrator, and not knowing if I would be allowed to continue as the basketball coach, a position that defined me at the time.

What I did know was that nobody would out work me, that I would remain positive no matter what, and I would immerse myself in the school community. I would like to say that my grit and the above-mentioned attributes helped to carry me through that year of not knowing what I didn't know.

That would be inaccurate though.

I was lucky enough to be in the right spot for me at that time in my career. I had the opportunity to work with a man of utmost integrity and intelligence. The principal of the building, Paul, had an endless amount of patience with me, as I seemed to be going to his office before pulling the trigger on any decision. I remember my wife at the time (ex-wife now) getting angry with me one time as I headed to the bathroom with a laptop in hand, and blurting out "Do you need Paul to help you wipe your butt?"

I know I went to Paul often and he certainly taught me the nuts and bolts of being a school administrator, but he also taught me something far more valuable: listen, learn from, and empower others.

When he first told me that, I asked if he meant the teachers. He said, "Yes, and the custodians, and the secretaries, and the school nurse, and the parents."

He smirked a bit when I asked about giving voice to the annoying and negative custodian who was working with us at the time. "Ok maybe not him, but you know who we should listen to the most?"

I was sure he was going to say the Superintendent so when he said, "the kids" I was a bit surprised. As a new administrator and still a shade under 30, this was the first time I had heard the importance of giving students a voice. I now realize how sad that is and how our education system could be so much better if we just listened to kids more. Why, in 2019, do will still too often follow the old adage of kids should be seen and not heard?

I like to think of myself as a collaborative leader who learns from the knowledgeable and creative teachers I have had the opportunity to work with over the years. The ability to listen and learn from the individuals you lead is a mindset, a skill to be developed over time. I have struggled with this challenge to listen more, talk less, try to see an issue from all angles, all perspectives. I would like to think I have gotten better at listening and learning from those I lead, yet I hope to do even better next year.

I have been enlightened to the fact that not everyone in a school brings the same skill set. Not everyone in a school is good at the same things. And, some do not fit the mold of what a traditional teacher should be able to do well. I see it as my job to find out where my teachers' strengths lie, what they are passionate about, and what motivates them. I see it as my responsibility to put them in a position to be successful, to be productive, and to be happy.

The way I figured this out was not by giving directives and demanding teachers jump through the same hoops, just because. It was by getting to know them, getting to know what drives them, getting to know what their strengths are, and trying to accentuate those strengths. This line of thinking was challenged early in my principalship when one of my best teachers handed in a plan book that was not up to par. This was someone who was kid-centered, love hands on activities, got her students thinking to not only answer questions, but to ask them as well. This teacher passed my ultimate litmus test...I would put my own kids in her class.

Her plan book didn't have much substance and it seemed pretty obvious that she had put it together as an afterthought. I know the importance of good planning when trying to deliver a solid lesson. I would plan my basketball practices down to the second and when I didn't, my practices were not as productive as I knew they could be.

This presented a bit of a conundrum. I knew this teacher was delivering each and every day, but her plan book? Not so much. I knew I couldn't give false praise, so my feedback went something like this, "Although your plan book is a bit thin, our school is lucky to have a teacher like you who embraces student-centered learning, provides her students with specific feedback, and makes learning fun!' We joked about it later and she let me know how happy she was to be called thin!

I could walk into her room at any time and she could tell me in detail what her plan was, what her goals were for her students, and how she would asses if they had gotten there. Were my goals and objectives for her in her classroom and as part of our school community met? You bet! In my mind it wouldn't make sense to insist she took extra time to write meticulous notes in her plan book for my benefit. The results would have meant more time on paperwork and less time on honing the craft of teaching. When I asked how she was able to stay organized and give her students what they needed, she took me to a back office in her science lab that had an elaborate filing system with different lessons, activities, and ideas aligned with the District's 6th grade science curriculum.

I want my teachers to be good teachers. This teacher was a good teacher; she was able to show me her plan, just in a different way. All I had to do was ask. It seems absurd to me to penalize this teacher just because she wasn't good at filling out my planning book template and I am sure all of my teacher friends are nodding their heads up and down.

Shouldn't we afford our students the same consideration? Why then do we penalize students for not jumping through the hoops we design, even when they meet all of the goals and objectives we have laid before them? Often, students are made to do hours of meaningless homework on topics they have already mastered. Then, we claim that we are teaching responsibility.

Was I letting my teacher off the hook because I was ok with her lame plan book?

What did I want her to do? Be a great teacher.

Was she? Yes!

Yet, as adults, we forget to provide kids with the same logical approach that we expect. You didn't do your homework on polynomials, zero for you, even though you can solve polynomials in your sleep and are able to demonstrate that skill on the test.

I understand there has to be some accountability, but if we had honest and open conversations with our students like good administrators do with their teachers, I truly believe we would see achievement improve, responsibility increases, and an overall better educational experience. Let the class know straight up exactly what it is you expect them to master. Talk about different ways to get there. Let it be an open discussion with the class, ask for ideas, ask for feedback, be flexible.

Some students may be reluctant to speak in a large group; try a Google form asking for feedback, or, better yet, have a quick one on one conference with your students laying out the plan for success. What is the best way for them to master solving polynomials? It could be offering some videos or podcasts that can be watched at home, some practice problems, a friend that could help them. It doesn't matter how students obtain knowledge, just that they do. Doesn't this method better teach responsibility than just assigning a bunch of problems for homework with consequences if they are not completed?

Whose responsibility is it that students learn what they are supposed to learn? It is a team effort: the teacher, the student, and the administrator. You may notice that I do not include parents. It is not that I don't think parents could and should support student success, it is just that so many parents are unable or unwilling to help in the education process for a variety of reasons. More often than I would like to admit, I have blamed the parents for their child's academic shortcomings. That was until I realized my kids don't pick their parents and certainly cannot control the amount of support they get. The best educators understand this, don't make excuses about inadequate parenting, and figure out a way to make sure the students are able to get what they need despite their station in life.

I am not sure why our education system does not value what students have to say more. Many kids go to school every day without a clear picture of what it is they need to do to be successful or more importantly why. Are we worried that when we give students a say in their education that we will lose control?

My answer to that is YES!

And we should lose control. When I say lose control I don't mean kids running and screaming through the hallways slugging beers, but I do mean students having a clear understanding of goals and objectives, with the teachers serving as a guide on how to get there. Students should question the how, the why, the when. They should question "the way we do things around here" Without that type of thinker, how can we expect our society to grow?

It is easy for an administrator to say give students a voice to the teachers, but I wanted to practice what I preach so I created a student advisory group with my superintendent. It turned out to be one of the best things I did all year. We started by designing a Google form in which students applied for admittance into the group. Our goal was to have two or three students from grades nine through twelve to make up a diverse group of students that would be a cross section of our high school student body. We didn't want just the high academic flyers; we wanted special education students, English language learners, honor roll students, and students who needed academic support.

We met with the students monthly for the second half of the school year and continued the group into 2018-19. We will definitely keep this group beyond this year. The structure of our meetings was simple: some 'getting to know you' activities, leadership activities, and then a platform for the students to provide us with feedback on areas that the school could improve. The larger council broke off into smaller groups for action steps that the District could implement in an effort to make the High School a better place for all kids.

These meetings were often the highlight of my month. I looked forward to connecting with students on a deeper level, something I have missed since I moved from building principal to assistant superintendent. I worked hard to plan meetings that were worthwhile for the students who would be giving up time in their classrooms. We did exercises around group dynamics, subservient leadership, and the importance of communication. We discussed the importance of soft skills and nuisances such as looking a person in the eye, learning names, body language, and the power of the smile.

I would like to think that we helped to develop future leaders and that they learned valuable skills from myself and our superintendent, but what we learned from these amazing young men and women far exceeded any wisdom we passed to them. There is no doubt in my mind that I am a better leader today than I was last year this time in large part because of what I learned from listening--truly listening--to what these students had to say. It took some time to build trust and meaningful relationships, but once we did, what we learned opened our eyes and gave us a glimpse into the world of students.

It was shocking and embarrassing when one of the students told us that they could spend a whole year sitting next to a classmate and never have a meaningful conversation with them because "everyone is so worried about some ridiculous test." He wondered why more time isn't spent on things that matter like how to speak to people, how to be a good person, how to be a good teammate. "No one has ever even taught us how to write an email!" "You guys have pretty important jobs" he continued, "How important is it for you to talk to other people, to communicate and work with others?" This shook both my boss and I with the simplicity and truth in Francis's statement.

We spoke of the importance of embracing differences, shared the fact that every weakness has a correlation strength and retold a story we heard from Freak Factor author David Rendell about the founder of Kinkos who felt he would not be where he is today if not for his dyslexia. Upon hearing this story one of the students started to tear up. She shared that her whole life she had been trying to hide the fact that she had a learning disability and this was the first time that she thought of it as a difference, not just a weakness.

Interestingly enough, one of the breakout groups had decided to tackle the issue of student voice. They talked of inspirational teachers who actually asked them how they could do better as teachers, what worked and what didn't and how some even had them complete anonymous surveys to help them improve their teaching. I smiled inwardly as one of these "amazing teachers", "Armida" as they referred to him, was Gary Armida, my writing partner and co-author of this book.

This group came up with the idea to create a survey that they will make available to all teachers who wish to get feedback from students. The plan is to have this survey (Google Form) that can be used by teachers, for teachers (sorry no admins) who truly want to hear what students have to say. It will be available after the first marking period this fall. I am optimistic that many teachers will take advantage of this resource.

The last meeting with this group was held at a local Mexican restaurant. Our kids made us proud with how they conducted themselves, better than most adults in the restaurant. No cell phones, no rude remarks to waiters, just polite kids having a great meal, enjoying each other's company, and discussing ways to make our school a better place.

I always knew if you want to really find out what happens in schools, ask the kids, but now it was even more clear to me. These high schoolers made me realize that the ticket to a successful initiative, project, lesson, class, and school district is to get honest feedback from the clients themselves, the students. This realization drove me to not only try to have more conversations with students when I visit the buildings and classrooms, but to encourage my teachers to get feedback from students to help them improve their craft.

Many teachers are rule followers and feel they need to follow the prescribed road map that is set forth by building leadership, District leadership, and State Ed. I am realizing a big part of my job is to not only stress creativity, thinking different, breaking script, but encouraging it and demonstrating how it is often better for kids. This in part is accomplished by listening to our most valuable resource, our students.

I feel it is more important that teachers speak to their students individually and in small groups to find out what they need and truly think, not just what they think we want them to say. It is impossible to teach all of the standards that are laid out in the 13 years we are given with our kids, but it is not impossible to find out what every kid needs and do our damn best to give it to them. To me, that is what education is about and that is what the best educators do. They can't do it with guys like me getting upset because teacher x didn't get to unit 9 of the CKLA curriculum. The best teachers I know figure out what the most important skills and concepts their students need to master, tell them ahead of time, and work with the students to get there.

The best educators I know go to the playground and lunch table to talk to kids on their turf. The best educators I know plan field trips with students not for students. The best educators make the rules with the kids, not give them to kids. The best educators see schools for what they are, a cooperative effort to empower tomorrow's leaders to not only master core competencies, but also to think, question, dream, and embrace their "freak." The best teachers I know give students a voice and the best administrators do everything they can to put teachers in a position to make that voice count.

The Teacher

One summer, I bumped into a colleague in the main office of our high school. I was surprised to see this person in during a late July day. But, there she was, filling out forms for our District copy person. After exchanging pleasantries, I asked her what she was doing.

"Oh, I decided to be really organized next year and send everything out for copying now."

I replied, "that's a good idea so at least you know that you have the lit (literature) ready if and when you need it."

"Yeah, I'm doing that and I already have all of my unit tests, practice sheets, and essay assignments. I'm set for the year."

She was proud of herself. And, to some degree, I admired the fact that she cared enough to think about her whole year. It wasn't as if she didn't care about what she was teaching. She obviously thought about a yearlong plan. So, there is positive in all of that.

I was torn with how I should respond. As I said, I admired that she cared and, as a colleague in my department, I was happy about that. But, fundamentally, I disagreed with this approach for one simple reason: she didn't know her kids yet. And, because she didn't know her kids, how could she possibly know what they need to learn and how to assess them?

I had to ask.

"How do you know you'll actually use that? What if your classes need something different?"

As soon as the words came out of my mouth, I knew I had made her feel uncomfortable. She replied, "Well, it's the curriculum and the kids have to know all of that so that's what I am doing."

I didn't like that I upset her and made her defensive so I turned it around on me. "Oh, I know. I just can't do it like that. I'm not that organized. I like to see what the kids are and make it up from there."

"Yeah, I can't fly by the seat of my pants."

That last phrase is one that I hear quite a bit. People tend to throw that label on me and others like me who aren't beholden to the sacred curriculum, at least word for word. That's not to say that I don't follow standards. But, the route to get kids to achieve those skills laid out in the standards and, more importantly, go beyond them will vary. It will vary from year to year. It will vary from class to class. It will vary from student to student.

All of this comes down to why you decided to become a teacher. What is your main goal? Is it to deliver the curriculum? Or, is it to prepare students to be active thinkers, inquisitive, problem solvers, and a person who could advocate for themselves? I choose the latter.

I believe that my classroom is charged with:

- Creating an environment where students can find their passions.
- Creating an environment where students feel comfortable to question the standard, question practices, and question my methods.
- Creating an environment where students have a voice in what and how they were learning.
- Creating an environment where students feel empowered and that what they have to say matters.
- Creating an environment where students know they are writers and that their words could change the world.
- Creating an environment where students could demonstrate skills learned through their own passions and interests, not through prescribed methods and templates.
- Creating an environment where students could be leaders while also realizing that they were a part of something bigger.
- Creating an environment where the "final product" could take many forms.
- Creating an environment where failure is part of the process and to accept that learning is rarely linear. Failure and roadblocks happen during any process. Successful people learn from that and adapt their process to create a better final outcome.
- Creating an environment where students would look for more than one side of an issue. Successful people realize that there are multiple perspectives to any issue, idea, or concept.
- Creating an environment where we seek to validate information, not just take it because it was written or presented to the public.
- Creating an environment where we not only identify problems, but create solutions.

That seems like quite a bit, but all of it can be accomplished when you believe that your job is to help kids find their voice, their passions, while learning and polishing skills that will take them through the rest of their lives. I found that out during my second year of teaching, once again because of my department chair.

My 8th grade class had just finished reading To Kill A Mockingbird, the Harper Lee classic. I was still green when it came to assessments so I had given a lot of quizzes along the way. When it came down to the final assessment of the whole book, I felt that I had given enough traditional assessments and wanted to do something more creative. I came up with the idea of putting Boo Radley on trial for the murder of Bob Ewell. I stayed late, planning out every detail, down to the role of each student and my intended outcome.

Looking back, I'm actually not nauseous of this assignment that the younger me came up with. It is a good, creative way to discuss and assess one of the thematic elements of the book. In other words, did the kids get the message? While I would refine this quite a bit some two decades later, this wasn't too bad for a second-year teacher who still had no clue what to do.

That cluelessness would become apparent the next day after I unveiled to project. Most of the class was excited. All of them wanted to be the main players of the mock trial. It seemed like a hit. Then, one student came up to me after the period.

"Mr. Armida? Can I do something a little different?"

"You don't like the assignment?"

That's a defensive question for sure.

"It's not that, but I just don't like getting up and acting in front of the class and all that. Can I make a movie instead?"

If a kid asked me today, I would start helping him plan out his movie. But, the 23-year-old version of me wasn't quite ready for this.

"Let me think about."

There are worse responses, I suppose.

I went to my department chair and filled him in. I was a combination of angry and anxious. I put a ton of time in on this idea and I couldn't believe that a kid didn't like it. My department chair got right to the point.

"Why wouldn't you let him do it? He's going to show you the same skills that the other kids are going to show. You should offer that idea to the entire class. It's about showing they got your point, not about completing your specific task."

He told me he would support whatever I decided to do, but I did what I always did; I listened to him. The student was thrilled with his alternative. Kids found out about and asked if they could do the same thing. When I said that they would be allowed, two kids worked as partners, playing the parts of Atticus, Scout, Jem, and Boo Radley. The first kid made a great movie with his legos, including music. And, the mock trial kids did a great job. In fact, I still have the VHS from that year. For those too young, those were the things that movies were recorded on before DVDs. DVDs were the things movies were on before Netflix.

I learned quite a bit from that experience. Curriculum is a vehicle for kids to learn skills, not specific tasks that are often compliance based. Every class will not look the same, even if it is facilitated by the same teacher. It is incumbent on us, the teachers, to give students options so that they can demonstrate their mastery of a skill. It is why almost every assessment I give includes multiple options. And, the last option always reads: "If you have a different idea, come talk to me about it. I am sure we can work something out."

When students feel like they have a voice in what they will learn and how they will demonstrate their understanding, they will be more engaged. They will be more passionate, more thorough, more inquisitive, and more willing to battle through adversity. The learning process, whether it is the writing process, learning how to solve a math equation, completing a science lab, or learning about ancient Egypt, will eventually get to a roadblock. If the student is invested, they will endure, relearn, find another way, or topple over the roadblock.

The current buzzword for this is grit. The real word is inspired.

If the student is merely completing something out of compliance, most will simply give up.

The buzzword for this is lazy. The real word is uninspired.

Two decades later, this belief resulted in one of the best experiences I've had as a teacher. Because my students felt that they had a say over what they were learning and how they would go about exploring it, they were passionate and worked harder than I asked them to work. That isn't a credit to me; it is a credit to them working on skills by using their interests.

At the start of our course, a tenth grade English class, we surveyed for topics of interest. Students were asked about their passions. They were asked about issues that got them upset or issues they thought were important. At first, they weren't sure if I was looking for a specific answer. Many of them, who were so accustomed to being told what to do, were quiet until they saw that I was truly asking them for guidance in what content to deliver. Once they realized that they could truly voice their interests and passions, answers came fast and furious.

For the first foray into this type of thinking and learning, we decided that the class would choose a theme for everyone to work with. We would learn the skills of evaluating sources for bias, finding multiple points of view and multiple stakeholders in an issue, how to synthesize all of that information, how to make an argument, how writers construct arguments, how to work with a team, how to effectively communicate, how to identify limitations in research, and how to offer realistic solutions to problems. These were the skills that I needed to teach. It would have been easy for me to pick a topic that I thought they were interested in. But, allowing them to have a voice made for a much better experience.

Each of my three classes chose an area of social protest. One class chose the "Take a Knee" movement that was in the news with the NFL season. The other two classes chose to deal with feminism, but in two distinct ways. One chose about whether or not feminism was hurting or helping. The other chose to focus on the pay gap issue. The beginning of the year required more direct teaching as students needed to see a model of how to evaluate articles, perspectives, and motives. They needed to see a model of how to look at a piece of art as an argument or how to watch a satirical video and see the real purpose. All of those models and discussions were based on their chosen area of interest. They were in; they were constantly looking for more information because it was their idea. I was still teaching skills, but their voice gave me the access point.

After that early period of modeling, students were then left to truly experience the purpose of the course: to explore the world through their own passions. The first part of the course is about working with a team on larger issues. Students selected their own teams and began to formulate a group question or issue to solve. Since groups had their own choice, topics were varied. One group asked whether or not college athletes should be paid. Another asked whether or not doctors should be accountable for prescription drug abuse. Another asked if race influences the justice system. Another worked through the issues of gun control. And, there were so many more. Students were looking at issues that mattered to them. More importantly, they were being asked to be a voice in those issues as they must provide recommendations.

Once the groups chose their questions, each group member chose a perspective to explore the issue through. One group could have economic, historical, societal, and scientific perspectives while another group could have philosophical, environmental, political, and futuristic. The point is that every issue isn't just viewed through one perspective. Once students chose their perspective, they would research through that perspective and write a paper. Students would learn the concepts of peer-reviewed sources and how to find a balance of sources.

This was the portion of the course where the writer's workshop model kicked in. I would walk into class and students would be ready to conference about their writing. I would have 20 to 30 conversations each period about individual writing. We would talk about claim development, using sources properly, documenting those sources, and, yes, even go over some grammar once they were done with a draft. Individualized time with each kid, the exact opposite of a one size fits all.

Once students were done with their individual part, they returned to their group with information from their perspective. Groups then had to synthesize all of that information to come up with an eight to ten minute oral presentation. This portion not only taught about working with a team, but it also taught practical skills such as how to properly use media for presentations, how to prepare for an oral presentation, and how to effectively communicate the information. The groups then gave their presentation in front of an audience of their peers and then had to effectively respond to defense questions about their argument and their group process. How many professions would love for applicants to come to them with these skills already refined?

Even more important than all of that, students were thinking and challenging themselves. They were setting their own deadlines. They knew the end date, but they were given the freedom to find their own process. Those who support homework as a means of developing responsibility should see that this seminar method actually does develop responsibility. Students are responsible to themselves, to each other, and to the overall goals of the team. Students are responsible to manage their time, not given daily "do this for a grade by tomorrow" rote tasks.

At no point during this process did I tell them that they were wrong. I would challenge their thinking. I would ask a lot of questions. I would offer help with the skills of putting together a presentation and writing a paper. But, the whole process was predicated on the foundation that their voice was important. They drove the content. What they had to say mattered. We worked hard to create a relationship where they could tell me what I needed to do to help them and I could help push them to strengthen their voice.

All students have passions. All students need to develop the skills of gathering information, evaluating that information, and synthesizing that information. All students need to be able to develop and defend an argument. All students need to develop the skills of communicating that argument in multiple mediums. All students need to develop skills that allow them to be productive and accountable members of a team. No matter the subject matter, we owe it to kids to develop these skills. And, there are opportunities to do so in each area as long as the focus is on student voice.

Those are the skills. By using their interests and allowing students to have a say in their learning activities, the quality of work, their creativity, and, most importantly, their interest was quite high.

Every classroom in every subject area can utilize this way of exploring. Social Studies teachers can use their curriculum to have students explore issues of a time period and apply either apply an argument to that particular time period or to today's world. Science can explore issues in the field in the same way. Even Math can show the practicality of learning concepts rather than just having students complete worksheets.

As a teacher of writing, it is my mission for students to be able to develop their voice. They must be given a canvas to truly develop their own voice rather than produce a product that they think I would like. This can only be accomplished by allowing students to choose their subject matter, much like the seminar class setup described earlier.

But, it goes far beyond that. Too often, voice is minimized before it is even given a chance. Far too often, attempts at writing instruction become correcting, rather than developing. Ideas matter. How students express them matter. We cannot give students a fill in the blank model where a class of 30 is essentially handing in the same piece of writing. Instead, we must allow students to create. We must conference with them and give feedback as to how to amplify their voice in order to make their ideas come alive. We must talk with them, hear their ideas, give them alternative ways to develop those ideas whether that comes in the form of maker activities, sketchnoting, talk sessions, or scene building activities.

What they have to say matters. We must develop that environment so that they feel empowered to speak their truth. Our conversations with them can help them refine, reflect, and become even more empowered. The majority of the writing process should be centered around ideas, structure, and how to best utilize their voice. Yes, grammar is a part of that, but it is not the focus of the writing process. It is one of the final parts and should be relegated to that part. Too often, grammar impedes ideas from being developed and brings down student confidence, thus muting voice. Once everything else is in place, grammar is addressed.

Writing instruction must focus on what students want to say, not what we want them to say. Yes, that requires a lot of one on one time, but isn't that the best form of education out there? With each conversation, their trust in us grows. Their confidence grows. Their willingness to take risks and/or play with their writing grows. They are more receptive to grammar corrections because they are invested and confident in their piece. All of this allows their voice to grow. When that happens, magic happens.

When you empower kids to take chances and to know that their voice matters, their writing goes beyond the classroom. Here are the first two paragraphs from a piece written by a freshman, who was writing about grade culture in schools.

> *Zero to one hundred. We are defined by a number.*
> *A number that will tell me I'm not good enough. A number that pushes*
> *me over the edge, drives me insane, and causes me, a fourteen-year-old*
> *girl to have mental breakdowns every week. Striving to get that one*
> *hundred, a perfect score is what's going to set you above the rest.*
> *Or so I'm told.*

There's passion in those words. There's meaning in those words. Much work and thought were put into formulating those words and structuring the piece. There was discussion, revision, and, yes, even some grammar work. But, those words--those ideas--were important to this young writer. Those are words that can, in conjunction with what followed in the piece, move people to make a change or, at the very least, realize that there is a problem with how grades are held over kids' heads.

By allowing students to choose to investigate areas of interest, by exposing them to different writing techniques and then letting them choose what suits them as writers, they can use their voice to change the world.

Another way to give students a voice in learning is to simply ask them for feedback. And, we should be asking for feedback quite often. Kris (The Admin) already discussed setting up a survey for teachers. I am proud to work for and with an administrator who would provide kids and teachers with a safe place in order to not only give students a voice, but to improve the classroom experience.

For me, even after 20 plus years, I am always trying to shake the feeling of "I could've done more" or "I could've done this better." For a while, I always thought those feelings were a sign that I wasn't a good teacher. That was until I had a conversation with a colleague, a veteran teacher of our 8th grade. She is the type of teacher you would want your child to have. She helps other teachers by sharing her excellent work. She is constantly offering to help the department in any way. She is a master of the curriculum, but, more importantly, she connects with each and every kid. I often get her students two or three years later at the High School. And, they all still talk about how special her class was. So, when she said that she still has feelings that things didn't go as well as she wanted and is constantly feeling like she could've done better, I knew I was in good company.

We all want to get better at our craft. One of the easiest and most efficient ways to get better is to get feedback from the students. Their voice can definitely have a positive impact on instruction. To learn more, I ask more. Throughout the year, I will ask students for feedback on lessons and units.

That whole course I just explained earlier? I remember after that first unit, I felt terrible. I sat in my office and wrote down a dozen things I could've and should've done. I do this because before asking for their feedback, I want to show them that I am reflective. I remember standing in the doorway, reading off my list of things I need to improve upon. Some were in disbelief that I was saying critical things about my teaching. Others tried to hide their nodding heads. Either way, my doing so opened up a dialogue for them to voice their experiences. After a discussion where they offered suggestions, we came up with a new plan for unit two. And, it was better because they had a say in it.

At the end of every year, I always give a course evaluation. It is important for me to hear what kids have to say. I want to know what they thought was great. I want to know what they thought was awful and/or a waste of their time. The only way I can know is to ask them.

It is never a waste of time to ask students what they think about your teaching or your class. If you provide a safe place and give the proper questions, students can provide tremendous, in-depth feedback that will improve your instruction and make your classroom better for your next group of kids. If you truly want to get better, evolve, and become a more effective educator, you must be willing to hear it all–the good, the bad, the ugly, and the downright nasty ugly. That information is vital, but is often overlooked. We need to make it a regular practice to ask kids about their time in a classroom.

During the year and at the end of the year, I will give a survey. This allows for each student to be heard. During the year, I can adjust my instruction on the fly. At the end of the year, I take their feedback and try to improve for the new group of kids.

My Survey Model

Anonymous

You are more likely to hear the truth when a kid knows that they can keep their identity private. That keeps the worry about grades out of a student's mind. Even though you would never do it, it is natural for anyone to think that. Think about when an administrator asks you to complete a survey. If your name is on it, you do think twice or word things differently.

Short Answers Are Valuable

We have this bad trend in the education field that puts quick data as more valuable than actual feedback. Sure, you could probably Google a quick survey with multiple choice answers such as "highly effective" and a range down to "not effective", but what are you really gaining? Ask kids questions; let them write their answers. Their answers can give you a clue about so many things, not just the question you are asking.

Here's an example of some excellent feedback from the question "What was the area that needed the most improvement in this class? Why?"

I would've liked if before the research papers started, we read samples of research papers and pulled them apart and analyzed those instead of spending so much time focused on how to identify reliable sources, bc writing the papers, I personally mostly just used EBSCO, which were all reliable/peer-reviewed.

When I started the research papers, I found myself not understanding the direction the paper had to go and the tone I had to establish. I was confused because I had never written a research paper so I would've liked reading more examples of good research papers.

There's so much to this answer and it will definitely impact how I approach this type of research paper next year. I will still place importance on reliable sources because that is important in today's world, especially when they don't have a database handed to them. But, showing them more specific models that demonstrate argument research papers will be more of a focus. We focused on models of research papers, the mechanics of it, but the tone and direction, in hindsight, wasn't done until later. Next year, it will be done earlier.

Without allowing students to actually write and give extensive feedback, I would've overlooked the nuances of writing. Covering that earlier in the process will make it far more effective. And, even though it wasn't a main point of the feedback, I will make a point to explain why reliable sources are important, even with the safety net of EBSCO.

Ask Them What They Wish
I always want to know what kids would've liked to learn in class. A lot of the times, kids will give titles of books that they wished to have read or activities they would've liked to have completed.

Ask Them What Activities They Did and Didn't Like
Your favorite lesson on your favorite book may not have resonated with kids. If you get enough negative feedback, it is probably time to revamp. Or, maybe it's time to pick something that may resonate more with kids. If you get kids to buy in, maybe you can bring in your favorite activity to show the relationship. It's easy and gratifying to read about the stuff kids dug, but it is equally important to hear what things didn't interest them. Then, you can decide whether the lack of interest outweighs the intentions of the lesson.

Ask About Your Style of Teaching
Yes, this can be sensitive. But, wouldn't you rather know if your way of doing things is effective? If enough kids say they are confused or needed something

else, you must change. Changing is difficult, but if your goal is to reach kids, you must be willing to hear feedback and evolve.

Ask Anything You Feel Could Help

Are you curious about a particular lesson and it's lasting power? Ask. Do you want to know if students feel like your grading practices are fair? Ask. If you can create an environment where students are free to give honest feedback, you can get valuable feedback on every area of your instruction. That is more valuable than a PD session or reading a book. This is first hand, practical feedback that directly applies to you and your audience. Sure, you may cringe at some things you read, but those moments are worth it because of the improvement it offers.

It has never been more important to develop young people who can use their voice in the world. That voice, however, needs the practical skills in order to be effectively heard and to know, exactly, what it is speaking out against. We need that for our future citizens. And, we already see this generation doing an excellent job of advocating for itself against a system that wants to keep them quiet. Our duty as an institution is to arm them with the skills of critical thought, the ability to identify agendas and bias, the ability to see more than their point of view, and the ability to craft and communicate an argument. We can use any literature or content as a backdrop for developing those important skills.

The only way to effectively teach those skills is to ask them. Students must be able to voice their passions and directions they want to take. With our guidance, we can utilize their passions to unlock a work ethic that will arm them with the skills to take on the world when they leave our classrooms. And, by asking them, we can improve our practices as well. We must create a classroom environment and a teacher-student relationship where they know that their thoughts are valued. And, we must show them that they are valuable enough to challenge their thinking as well as influence our actions in the room.

Student Voice Takeaways for Admins

+ If you want the adults in your building to provide students with a voice you must model that as a leader.
+ Find out what motivates those you lead and put them in a position that accentuates their strengths.
+ Provide students several platforms to provide the adults with honest feedback.
+ If you really want to know what school is like, ask the kids.
+ If you really want to know what works and what doesn't, ask the students.
+ Have honest and open conversations with students; they can smell BS a mile away.
+ Encourage students to be leaders today, rather than just leaders in the future.
+ Talk to the students on their turf, the playground, lunchroom, hallways, etc. remember the principal's office can be a scary place
+ Build authentic relationships with students. they will be more apt to provide authentic feedback.
+ Have high expectations for kids; they will usually rise to the occasion.
+ Treat kids with respect if you want respect reciprocated.

Student Voice Takeaways for Teachers

+ No matter the course or grade level we teach, our first priority is to help students find their voice.
+ Classroom practices can improve with the feedback provided by students.
+ Asking students to provide anonymous feedback will help give meaningful direction to classroom instruction.
+ Students learn best when they are passionate about the subject matter.
+ Students will be more invested if they have a voice in their work.
+ It is never a waste of time to ask kids what they think about your class and your style of teaching.
+ Feedback from students should be elicited as many times as possible during the year, not just as an end of the year activity.
+ Students should be given the opportunity to have a voice in how they demonstrate the skills learned.
+ Student writing should be a process in which their voice is the center. All skills taught should focus on strengthening their voice.
+ Grammar instruction has an important place, but it should always be the last part of the writing process. Ideas, voice, and structure are far more important.

VOICES FROM THE FIELD...
Angela Stockman, Teacher Coach, Writing Instructor

One of the first conversations that my first college professor had with my freshman Composition class was all about voice. Ours collectively, and mine, specifically.

I had no idea what he meant, of course.

Prior to this, no one spoke with me about my writing voice, other than to mention that I didn't have much of one. This seemed to be the least of my teachers' concerns, though. Structure mattered. The use of precise vocabulary words mattered. My spelling, punctuation, and mechanics mattered.

I didn't realize that voice mattered until suddenly, it did.

And this changed my entire life.

My freshman year of college introduced me to not one professor but an entire department full of professors who helped me find my voice by expecting me to use it--on the page, in class, and during their office hours as well. Thanks to them, I've reaped all of the rewards that any writing life can offer. I use it to advocate for my own needs and for others who have not yet found their own. I use it to teach. I use it to make people laugh. I use it to extend a bit of humanity to others who need it as well.

In recent years, I've learned more about the powerful role that empathy plays in our personal and our professional lives. I've learned how to practice it better, and through that learning, I've met teachers who are eager to do the same. Together, we're eager to access and listen to what children have to say about their wishes, their worries, and their wildest dreams. We design learning experiences this way.

How beautiful it is to pay my own learning forward in this way. The best teachers I've ever had were the ones who helped me find my voice. I'm trying to become a better teacher by helping teachers and children raise their own voices. And what I've realized is that accomplishing this is about so much more than what lands on a page, even though this is how my first and most formative experiences with voice began.

I continue to wonder how we might better access the voices of the students we serve, and how we might use what we learn from their contributions to craft curricula, plan instruction, and assess in ways that attend to their interests and their needs. When is it important to seek their perspective? How might we accomplish this in the most powerful ways possible?

How might this sort of work change education for the better?

4

Professional Growth

"Live as if you would die tomorrow. Learn
as if you were to live forever."
~ Mahatma Gandhi

The foundation is set. The Teacher and Admin team work together with parents to give students their voice. It sounds simple, right? But, there is an art to education. There is no one size fits all method that works for all kids. We must, as an industry, make every effort possible to add to that art. We must continually seek to find better, more engaging, more meaningful methods to reach every kid.

For administrators, the challenge is to provide teachers with meaningful, practical, and inspiring professional development. Professional days can no longer be about school business matters. They must focus on pedagogy, mindfulness, and pushing practices so they evolve to meet the needs of today's students and tomorrow's leaders. Administrators must be willing to send their teachers to conferences, have their teachers see other teachers and best practices, and open up opportunities to learn.

For teachers, the challenge is to view these days with seriousness and positivity. These days cannot be viewed as days off or opportunities to take a "harmless" day off. Teachers must have a growth mindset and come into each professional development opportunity with the idea that they can come out with at least one thing that they can bring back to their classrooms. Teachers must also be willing to open their classrooms so that colleagues can see their methods and learn from each other. Much like we want our students to be lifelong learners, we educators must continue to learn and be seekers of knowledge.

The Admin

A school's greatest resource is the people who walk the halls, who bring the classrooms to life, and who give their hearts and souls to our youth. Our primary focus should be on cultivating and growing that talent. If we are asking our teachers to evolve as educators, leaders must evolve as well. It is time to take a different approach to professional growth in our education system.

One of the most successful businesses in the world, Amazon, lists "hire and develop the best" as one of their core leadership principles for success.

"Googler" Rachel Gillett describes her experience working at Google "as a transformational experience. Professionally, you are constantly growing and evolving by tackling the most complex challenges imaginable and learning from your peers. Personally, you are surrounded with the type of knowledge, talent, and passion that inspires you to do things that matter — to you and to society as a whole."[2]

If you work at Amazon or Google your work experience is much different than that of most employees of a public school system. Lunches are not a choice between Sloppy Joes and over cooked frozen pizza complete with a side of sugar infused peaches that come from a giant can rather than a tree that basks in the sunlight. Coffee is plentiful, and you are not expected to put a dollar 50 in a jar every time you pour a cup of bitter burnt mess, risking the glare of the overworked cafeteria lady every time you do not have cash readily available.

---

2 Gillett, Rachel. "Here's What It's REALLY like to Work at Google the 'World's Most Attractive' Employer." *Business Insider*, Business Insider, 6 Sept. 2015, www.businessinsider.com/heres-what-its-really-like-to-work-at-google-the-worlds-most-attractive-employer-2015-9.

The work environment at the world's most successful companies is one in which you are expected to work hard, one where you will be treated with respect, and one with the freedom to work how you need to work. You will grow, you will learn, you will experiment, you will take risks, you will think in ways that others have not yet thought.

At the Google's and Amazon's of the world, different is not only accepted, it is revered; the expectation is you keep up, you evolve, or you are shown the door. If we are expected to get students "College and Career Ready" for success in today's ever-changing world it is time to change how we instruct our students and the only way to do that is to change how we cultivate and grow our teachers.

Our greatest resource is our employees. Our clients are the students. It is time to think differently about how we treat, grow, and develop our talent. Our clients' success is more important than success in any other business. Doctors save lives, educators shape lives. Judges (hopefully) ,make rulings based on ethics, educators develop ethics. Amazon makes our lives more convenient, educators make life worth living.

The most important job in the world is that of an educator. Educators are responsible for ensuring our future citizens are healthy emotionally and physically, are thoughtful, are creative, are fulfilled, and are the type of people we want to live in and shape our world.

We must treat them differently, pay them differently, and support their professional growth differently. We must listen to them, respect them, and believe in them, if we want them to do the same for the students they serve.

Often times, doing it takes courage, but it also takes logic. Why not have a decent cup of coffee available at no cost for those of us who need our afternoon caffeine fix?

Why not have decent lunch options available?

Why not allow time in the day for walking, wellness, mental health breaks?

THE **TEACHER** & THE **ADMIN**

The perception that if we spend too much time and money on these "fringe" benefits, we are wasting "taxpayer money". This type of thinking is a perfect example of penny wise and dollar foolish. It will cost much more in the long run when we have educators who are not at their best, who miss time due to illness, who do not feel respected, who are exhausted, who are stressed, who are on overload. Pay me now or pay me later, but, eventually, the cost will come and our students are much too valuable to have that cost be at their expense.

We must get professionals excited to grow, learn, evolve, take risks. When teachers are expected to or continue to teach the same way for 30 years our students suffer. Would you want a doctor who has not grown in the last 30 years? Would you buy your child a Commodore 64 as they head off to college? We grow, we evolve, we get better--so should educators.

When we embrace change and improvement it does not mean that what we did in the past had no value; it does not mean that we were a failure or what we did was a failure. Rather, it means that we evolved like the world around us, that we improved, became better, more open, more inclusive. That we built the foundation, a higher starting point for those that come after us.

Is it a wonder that so many teachers burn out or leave the field? Can you imagine doing the same thing day after day, year after year in the same room, teaching the same outdated and often times overwhelming mandated curriculum, all the while paying a $1.50 for terrible coffee?

Lucky for the field, things are changing and the one size fits all strategy for growing our professionals in no longer the norm.

We are seeing less and less of the following practices that are more about conformity and "the way we do things" than true professional growth.

- Everyone doing the same thing the same way
- Trying to do too much in one session
- Not providing time to reflect and work with information
- Providing too many dittos and papers
- Making it all about test scores
- Relying solely on data

- Boring sessions
- Relying on PowerPoints
- Providing information rather than encouraging thought
- My way or the highway attitudes from administrators
- Letting the loudest most argumentative voice dominate sessions

When I look back at some of the strategies I have used in the past to grow those I led, I often cringe. I thought it was necessary to solve all the ills in my school in one, hour-long faculty meeting, cramming every second with all of the tips and tricks I learned at the latest conference or book I read. I now know it is better to focus on one or two key concepts, ideas, or skills.

I now know it is better to spark interest, to open minds to different possibilities.

I felt it was necessary to have teachers answer my guided questions if I asked them to work independently. I now know it is better to model, call out, and practice the type of protocols that lead to productive professional conversations, then entrusting teachers to have those conversations.

I worried that if there was no consistency in practice that students will suffer. I now know that when we take the art out of teaching, when we try to jam teachers into the same box, when we do not embrace teachers who are courageous enough to do things differently, students will suffer.

Most districts do not have enough faculty meetings, staff development days, substitute teachers to cover days out of the classroom, the resources to spend on conferences. That being said, district and building level administrators can work to develop a culture of learning, a culture of respect, a culture that encourages risk-taking, supports collaboration, and embraces those who are brave enough to be different.

Professional Growth Sessions

It may be a faculty meeting, a department meeting, a committee session, or any other opportunity to facilitate professional growth. Regardless of what it is called, any time a group of educators is together it is a chance to grow and develop the craft we love and have important philosophical conversations that can help to move the organization in the right direction.

I have found it effective to open these sessions with a welcoming activity to get the participants in the right mindset to grow as professionals. Even the most confident presenters can experience butterflies or self-doubt when starting a session some may perceive as too "kid like" or "Elementary." In my experience, once you get past the groans and eye rolls, everyone gets into it and enjoys the learning.

I have more recently used mindfulness techniques to open. Pointing to the research Harvard[3] is conducting in the area of mindfulness can be a good way to hook even the most cynical participants.

Welcoming Activities to Get Participants Ready to Learn:

4 Square breathing - Lead the group by drawing a square with your finger up to a count of four, across and hold to a count of four, down and out to a count of four, across and pause to a count of four. Repeating four times is enough to reset our minds and get us ready to learn. You can also utilize this exercise by yourself by simply drawing the square on a paper to the same count.

Guided Meditation - There are plenty of guided meditation exercises on YouTube. Simple search guided meditation and the length you desire. It is easy to find several you like. One of my favorites is "The 5 Minute Vacation"[4]. Let the group know there is nothing for them to do other than to listen to the mediation session. Dimming the lights can help to set the mood. Hit play, sit back and just be with your group.

Mindful Music - Play a song of your choice, and ask your audience to close their eyes and listen to the words, instruments, and rhythm. A quick "turn and talk" to debrief is a great way to realize how much we notice and often miss.

I truly believe in the benefits of mindfulness, but not everyone is ready for

---

3 Powell, Alvin, and Alvin Powell. "Harvard Researchers Study How Mindfulness May Change the Brain in Depressed Patients." *Harvard Gazette*, Harvard Gazette, 27 Aug. 2018, news.harvard.edu/gazette/story/2018/04/harvard-researchers-study-how-mindfulness-may-change-the-brain-in-depressed-patients/.

4 HeartsEssence. "The 5 Minute Vacation." *YouTube*, YouTube, 7 Oct. 2008, www.youtube.com/watch?v=3LAmYS6kb7k.

mindfulness and not all facilitators are comfortable leading a mindfulness exercise. I have found some of these simple activities effective as well for setting the stage for a successful session:

The Best - Have the group write down the best thing that happened to them today, this week, this year. They can then share at their table or with the group.

Reading - It is easy to forget how fast everyone is moving and we never have enough time to just sit in silence and read. Choose a few relevant articles to pick from, or, better yet, have your group search for one they may like. Then provide 5-10 minutes of silent reading time.

Around the World - Pose some questions on poster paper hung throughout the room. The questions should be simple, but thought-provoking. The group moves "around the world" answering the questions and reviewing the responses of others. Some examples:
Describe a time you made a difference.
What is the quality you most respect in a leader?
What is something new you want to learn?
What is your favorite tech tool?
How do you connect with students?
What is the nicest thing a colleague has ever done for you?

Grateful game - Each participant has a scrap piece of paper. 45 seconds is put on the clock and the facilitator calls out a topic. The group has to write as many items they are grateful for in the category called. You can cycle through 4 or 5 categories and add some spice by giving a small prize or a pat on the back to the person who gets the most. Some topics of gratitude can be:
- Food
- Nature
- People
- Books
- Movies
- Experiences
- Reasons for being an educator

Most of these activities take less than five minutes and the benefit of having the group in the right frame of mind is well worth the time.

After the opening, it is essential to review the agenda for the day and what the goal of the session is. Just like what we expect from our teachers when they work with students, we should be clear, concise, and simply state what it is we are trying to accomplish and avoid eduspeak at all costs.

It is easy to fall into the trap of trying to do too much or over-complicating things. I ask myself "if they leave with one or two things, what should that be?"

I have learned through the years that no matter what the topic is, what the learning is, people need time to think, reflect, and process. "Turn and talk" or discuss at your table are great ways to quickly debrief, yet sometimes it is beneficial to ask individuals to reflect on their own before sharing with the group (Think, Pair, Share). A one or two-minute timer to jot down some thoughts allows all attendees to think before the loudest, most confident voices speak.

The best professional development sessions I have run are the ones that allow my teachers and administrators to think, reflect, move, and work with the content I am providing.

It is essential to make the information relevant to the work that the educators we are trying to grow do on a day to day basis. The best leaders stay connected, stay grounded, and understand that the best techniques, tools, ideas, and resources only work when the practitioners have time to apply it to the work they are doing.

The best leaders also realize that what may work for one educator may not work for another. It is our responsibility to recognize and support that fact.

Staff Development Days

Districts do not have enough staff development days to accomplish all that needs to get done. Unfortunately, this often creates a pitfall where administrators try to do too much and teachers leave feeling resentful for the time missed with students.

In my district, we have over 600 teachers. That is a lot of moving parts. Trying to roll out a cookie cutter program or an initiative on one of these days would go over like a lead balloon.

I have tried to focus on providing our teachers with a philosophical message that can be motivating, entertaining, and can change some hearts and minds.

Based on anecdotal feedback and survey results, our teachers find value in this approach. When I brought in Dave Rendell, who is known for his penchant for wearing pink, his book Freak Factor, and his philosophy that every weakness can be a strength and every strength a weakness depending on the situation, our teachers burst out into a raucous standing ovation.

Not because Dave is an amazing presenter (which he is) or that his ideas are extremely relevant to the work we do in schools (they are), but because it was made clear to our teachers that this wasn't about a program, they didn't have to implement anything.

All they had to do was to think about the message and how it applies to their work. Three years later, teachers still mention Dave and how he changed how they approach their teaching practices and how they see their most challenging students.

Teacher choice, teacher led sessions, and time to work with grade level or subject colleagues have proved to be fruitful learning experiences during staff development days.

I find it challenging to let go of control, but when I do the learning is most effective.

People need time to build bonds, connect, talk, and think. It is ok to have some unstructured time for connection and overall wellness. Education is an important profession, an enchanting profession; it is essential that administrators treat the teachers they lead as the professionals they want them to be and our students need them to be.

It is also essential that teachers take ownership of their own development. The best administrative teams I know do all they can to support teachers in their personalized growth.

I have experimented with various learning opportunities for teachers that I hoped would help them get excited about improving at their craft--some successful and some huge failures. Despite striking out from time to time, I am always willing to take a chance because as all good educators know, not all learning happens the same way for the same people.

Approaches that I have found to be successful for some include:

Team Conferences - Taking a group or sending a group to State and national conferences. This can be a costly option, but hearing from leaders in the field, seeing the latest techniques, and building bonds with your team have proven to be worth the investment time and time again.

Different Learning Experiences - It is important to be creative when promoting learning for your staff. The same old PowerPoint year after year will not cut it. Switching up your presentation platform by using Prezi or Pear Deck can help. Showing videos to emphasize a point, tug at heartstrings, or add some levity are also ways to spice up your presentation. I have also utilized Poll Everywhere or Mentimeter to involve the audience in the learning.

Although these are all excellent ways to improve your presentations, I have found thinking differently and taking a completely different approach is even more valuable. Ideas from educators I have connected with on Twitter have sparked ideas as well as great books such as 4 o'clock Faculty and Gamestorming. I have found a wide variety of ideas that I have modified to make work for my style and my audience.

Some of my favorites are:

Picnic PD
Outdoor learning stations that participants rotate through. Adding a favorite picnic snack and table cloth to each station can add to the experience.

Learning Walks

Provide a few guiding questions, ask for thoughts on a speaker or presentation, and have partners walk, talk, and reflect on the information provided.

Book Tasting

This one was modified from Richie Czyz (4 O'clock faculty). I set up several stations with two books at each station, an information sheet which they can take notes on, and a few snacks at each station. When I am feeling more creative I add a theme for the day and decorate and snack accordingly. The groups have five minutes at each station to check out the books before they move to the next set of books. After reviewing all of the books they get to choose the one and take it with them. This approach also creates an organic book club.

Picture Scavenger Hunt

This can be done in groups or individually and the topics can vary depending on the goals and objectives you have set forth. Team building can be accomplished by taking pictures with students, staff members, or parents.

Want more awareness of the facility? Make pictures of different locations the requirement. Want them to get ideas from other teachers? Have them take pictures of great bulletin boards, class setups, or other ideas obtained by seeing other classrooms. The possibilities are endless.

Teacher Collaboration

Encouraging teachers to learn from each other is one of our field's most underutilized strategies. It can be covering classes so teachers can watch each other teach, exposing your educators to the connected world of amazing teachers on social media platforms such as Twitter or offering teacher lead learning sessions.

We have increased our professional learning network through our completely voluntary Twitter Challenge. Alos, started to make peer observations the norm through our Pineapple Challenge. One of our most well-received learning opportunities has been our professional development offerings catalog. Teachers and administrators submit a proposal to teach after school sessions. Teachers who attend the sessions are awarded In-service and CTLE credits.

Independent learning opportunities like digital badging can also help to give ownership to teachers in their professional growth.

As leaders and educators, we can get caught up in the hustle and bustle of the important work we do each and every day and forget to take the time to hone our craft. The best Districts, Administrators, and Teachers understand the value of professional growth and work to get better together.

The Teacher

I was in the copy room during that eventful first year of teaching. It was springtime and I was happy. I was surviving my first year of teaching, I was coaching baseball and the season looked promising. I had found my way with the students. Looking back now, I realize all of the mistakes I made, but I was always pro-kid and always looking out for them. All in all, things were good.

A science colleague came in and started talking about her classes. It was the typical stuff, just the normal copy room chit chat. We started to talk about what we were going to do with our classes that day. In passing, she said, "You're a good teacher."

I said thank you and returned the compliment. But, I remember being struck with the notion of someone thinking I was good. Did other people feel this way? I mean, how do they know?

Seriously, how do they really know?

Aside from the three observations, two of which were carefully planned, and that snooping first department chair who constantly reminded me how poorly I spoke, nobody really knew if I was any good. Maybe it was because I was good with kids and had positive relationships. That is the most important aspect of the job, but that doesn't necessarily mean I was a good teacher.

That sort of "good teacher" reputation followed. Maybe they were right, but I always would think that it was so weird that people would make a judgment about my competency in the classroom without ever really watching me.

The other part of that is the idea that districts rarely focused on improving the craft of teaching. I would say that the first dozen or so years of my career, the focus in faculty meetings and superintendent conference days were always focused on business and, maybe, some curriculum work. Pedagogy was never, ever a focus. Districts weren't too keen to shell out money for us to attend conferences. Even new teacher meetings focused on how to do the proper seven-page lesson plan, how to make sure you cover the curriculum, and how you should put kids in place so you have classroom order.

The monthly faculty meetings were glorified pep rallies, complaint sessions, and rule reminders that we teachers weren't implementing properly. That sort of set a tone for the industry when it came to professional development.

There wasn't any.

So those "PD" days became "easy days" where we could check out mentally. Our biggest worry of those days was how long our lunch was going to be and whether or not they were really going to keep us the full day.

It set a negative mindset, even when we had individuals who wanted to give more. When my first mentor took over our English Department in my second year of teaching, department meetings were about methods of teaching writing, differentiating all instruction, and ways to get kids own their work. But, most of the department tuned out. The profession didn't really create an environment of learning, of getting better, and genuinely trying to evolve. Sure, teachers would share plans and what they did in the room, but replicating a lesson plan isn't growth. It isn't learning a new strategy or connecting with kids. But, if you showed the slightest inclination of wanting to get better or learn something new as I did during our department meetings, you were viewed as someone who was kissing up to administration.

During my third year of teaching, we had an interim principal. He was a nice man who was gentle, quiet, and wasn't out to get anyone. He had this notion of teaching his staff. So, he relieved us of a team meeting once per week and brought us into a classroom. Each week was a particular skill, but his theme was always differentiated instruction. Looking back, there was a lot of good stuff and he was ahead of his time in terms of trying to improve pedagogy.

The problem is nobody listened. People sat, blatantly doing other things rather than listening to a man who was trying to make us better. In my group, we had the chief building union rep. On our way in one day, he bragged about not caring about this. "We (the union) let Larry have this little moment where he feels like a teacher. It keeps him quiet."

So, instead of even picking up one new strategy, we all just tuned out. Shame on us. Shame on me. I wish I was stronger then. If it were now, I would've reacted quite differently.

Thankfully, the focus of professional development has changed over the past five or six years. With the evolving requirements of maintaining a teacher license, there is now a premium on the idea of continuous learning. That not only benefits us in the classroom, but it truly benefits the kids that we teach. This focus has pushed the profession further, making us have those uncomfortable conversations about homework, about classroom practices, about aligning lessons to the demands that kids will face in the real world. Most importantly, it has made us think about doing better in the classroom.

But, there is a delicate balance when it comes to professional development and teaching. Teaching is an art. Yes, when done right, we do our research, we plan out units, and we know what is important to have kids learn. But, the "how" in all of this is really teaching. The "how" is an art. Artists--creators--need a level of arrogance when it comes to being great.

Arrogance is a negative word, usually. But, think about it. Performers, artists, writers, athletes, and, yes, teachers have this trait. It is needed in order to have the ability to perform in front of an audience, to think that people would want to see your creations, to have the audacity to think that your words would matter to the world, to think you can win a competition every time you step on a field, and to stand in front of a room full of kids and say, "I am a guide who can help your learning."

That quality drives a performer to rehearse and perform at his/her peak. It drives an artist to continually find new ways to express his/her point. It drives a writer to push his/her words to change the world. It drives the athlete to train harder so that he/she is ready to perform in pressure situations. And, it drives the teacher to know that he/she can guide a group of kids throughout the year.

That quality is precisely why professional development is so important and precisely why professional development is so difficult.

Let's start with the latter.

There is a sense of being in control in a classroom that a good teacher has. Nobody can do the job like we can. So, when you find something that works, it is often difficult to change or see that there might be an even better way. The good teachers have developed a process, worked at it, and found success with it. It is difficult to give up a process that was successful in the past.

I fought that quality for a long time, longer than I should have. Because I thought I had a good thing going, I had the "shut the door" mentality. Colleagues would talk, but I wouldn't advertise what I was doing and I wouldn't really ask what they were doing. I wasn't going to workshops. I wasn't really reading about new methods. Basically, I was stagnant. Sure, I would find something here and there or think of something different, but I wasn't growing. People thought I was a good teacher, but I was getting into perhaps the most dangerous territory a good teacher can get into.

Our Middle School Principal is one of the good guys. He's a former social studies teacher and is definitely insightful with people. He has a way of simplifying things, as you saw with Anthony Zollo's words in chapter two. He categorizes the teachers who are good, but not growing as "Living on Legend". Obviously, there are some really good qualities to these teachers. They are usually good with kids, can teach a sound lesson, and generally have a pleasant way about them.

But, these are the dangerous ones. These are the ones we have to watch for and help in our field. We have to watch out that we don't become one.

We know the people who are in it for the wrong reasons. We know the damage they can do. We can minimize their damage. We know the ones who are constantly trying to improve. We can help them. But, the Living on Legend

Teachers can do a lot of damage to kids before anyone realizes that they are still doing worksheets from the 1980s and aren't pushing kids further in the writing process or any other skill development. We want our good colleagues to continue to grow, to continue to push, and to continue to innovate. That not only benefits kids, but it furthers our field.

Instead of the arrogance of "shutting my door and doing my thing," we must be mindful of that arrogance and use it to push us to get better, to challenge ourselves to address our weaknesses, and to challenge ourselves to continue to innovate, even if it means letting go of treasured lessons. We must have the mindset of our performers, our artists, our writers, and our athletes. Our arrogance must drive us to continue to improve. To improve, we must embrace professional development.

How do we do that?

Find Your Crew

First, it is important to find your crew. Your crew is a group of professionals that make it ok to like the job, that makes it ok to sit and plan things or to talk about wanting to get better. There is an undercurrent in our system that makes it difficult for some to say that they like the job or to show that they care about the students. There is a lot of that noise and it is our job to mute those naysayers and find a group of people who make it ok to want to sit and plan, who make it ok to want to get better, to do more, and to be more. In order to get the most out of professional development and your career, you must surround yourself with people who share that same mindset.

There was a point about ten years into my career where I thought I wanted out. Looking back, I wasn't surrounded by the right people during that time. I wanted to find a job writing about sports. But, the reality was, I was bored. I was stuck teaching the same type of lessons year after year. I wasn't getting better. I always hung onto the relationship part with kids; that was the only thing that kept me coming back. But, I wasn't moving forward with my instruction, often loading up disks with the previous year's plans and activities. The problem is that the "previous" year became two years ago, then three years ago.

Like most things in my life, I lucked into a friendship with a social studies colleague. He was actually writing baseball with me, but he had a different focus. Baseball writing was his creative outlet; his innovation in the classroom was always first. The more I hung out with him, the more I saw him push past the typical lecture model of a typical social studies class. He pushed project-based learning, real-world activities. I'd see him not only connect with kids, but continue to innovate.

Our conversations evolved from just baseball to the classroom. When our Principal asked us to create that 9th grade program, it not only helped kids, but it sparked in me the need to innovate. Doing something new was invigorating. Having someone who was willing to sit down and plan, talk about teaching and the desire to do well so freely made me better.

Around this same time, another colleague, this one from my department, began to come in and just talk. Even when my door was closed, she would be the only one to come in. We'd talk about philosophy, the real purpose of teaching literature, how to move the department forward, issues in education, and what we can do better for kids. While we weren't planning lessons, we were bouncing ideas off of each other. I was shifting my focus to the real purpose of teaching; I began going less and less to those disks with old stuff. I was creating again. I was developing.

Those two relationships gradually made me more outgoing about how I felt about the profession and how I wanted to get better. My conversations changed with many of my colleagues. One would text me or call me to run her lesson ideas by me. Even though she has been teaching for 24 years, she continues to plan and innovate. Just talking with her will inspire new ideas to use in the classroom.

Because I am now willing to talk about how I feel about the job and how I want to get better, the crew has gotten bigger. There are more of us out there than bad ones. As my crew grows, the profession gets better because we are not just sharing lesson plans. We are discussing the process, the reason, as well as the execution of what we teach. With this, I am no longer just in a classroom. I am a part of something bigger, doing something bigger. As a result, kids are getting a better, more useful education.

The "One Thing" Mentality

Having those discussions with your crew is important. But, professional development is more than that. We, as educators preparing students to take on the world, must actually see more than just our colleagues. It is vital to go to conferences, participate in workshops, and genuinely listen when guest speakers and presenters are brought to your district. There is always something that can make you a better practitioner, a better planner, or a more compassionate teacher.

Again, we must use that arrogance to drive us to want to learn from others and not just sit in a session with an "I already know this" or "I can do this better" attitude. It is a difficult mentality to develop because as teachers we feel that we know our kids best, we know what works, and we know how to guide our kids. How can some outsider possibly know better?

But, that's the thing we have to avoid. We have to avoid the mindset of thinking that a professional development session is someone else telling us how to do something. It isn't that at all. The mentality should be about getting more tools or more perspectives to add to the toolbox so that when you go into a classroom, you have more resources.

Mike Trout is the best player in Major League Baseball. In his seven full-time Major League seasons, he has won two Most Valuable Player Awards, the honor for being the best player for that season. In four other seasons, he finished second, while finishing fourth during a season in which he missed time due to injury. Those second place finishes could've easily been first place finishes because his statistics were better than the players who won the awards those particular seasons. It is a remarkable accomplishment for a player to be that consistently elite considering the competitiveness of Major League Baseball.

Yet, Trout is always the first person at the ballpark, getting extra practice, working on his swing. He will pick one thing to work on during each session, whether it is to hit to the opposite field, work on his launch angle, or tweak his mechanics, he works to get better. Instead of just being satisfied with being elite, he continues to work harder than everyone else. Before last season, he stated that he wanted to be more patient and more efficient. The result? A career high in walks--a total that led the league--and the most efficient baserunning season of his career.

The elite always look to get better. The elite always look for one thing to improve upon.

Professional development should be taken that way by teachers. What is one thing that I can do to make my teaching better for kids?

A few years ago, my district was looking for a way to improve our writing practices. The Admin and I did our research. We went to conferences. We investigated programs and people. At one point, I said, "Just let me do it."

I was confident in my writing instruction; it was one of my strengths. I genuinely felt I could do it well. Kris didn't say anything to me when I said it.

Later that day, he called me.

"Gary, I really need you on board with this. I know you're a great teacher, but I think having another voice along with yours will move us forward."

I trusted him. And, I am glad I did because it led to working with Angela Stockman. When Angela first began working with our department, the majority were a little resistant. Again, it is always difficult to have an outsider come in and tell you how to teach your kids. But, Angela wasn't doing that. She was giving us process ideas. She was giving us tools. For those of us who were open, we instantly gained such great teaching tools for writing.

I employed my "one thing" philosophy during our sessions. At the start, I knew that I needed help with topic generation for students. I really disliked just handing kids a topic to write about or giving them a list. So, during Angela's sessions, I would focus on anything and everything in regards to topic generation. And, that strategy worked. It allowed me to avoid the "I do this too" and really focus on getting something I really wanted to improve upon.

During every professional development session atend, I go in with a focus.

What is one thing I want to get out of it? Obviously, the quality sessions---like Angela's---there will be more than one thing to get. But, there are sessions that can be underwhelming. Not every presenter is engaging. Not every presenter is organized or tells you something life changing. But, if you go into the session with a "one thing" mentality, the time is well spent. You can get one thing out of every professional development session you attend, even if it is something small. You can head back into your classroom with one more tool in the toolbox that can help a student.

Stay Engaged: Take Notes

I learned this from the Admin. I was always the one who would go into a session and just listen. I am someone who can listen, filter, and get the gist of what is going on. The first time I went to a conference with Kris was when he took a group of us to the ASCD conference. We sat for one of the keynote speakers. It was Todd Whitaker. I was ready to listen when I got a notification that Kris shared a document with the group. I opened up the document and saw that he was taking these really detailed notes of Whitaker's presentation. As we listened, I saw Kris adding pictures, capturing key phrases, embedding videos, and adding some of his own thoughts about how he would use some of the stuff presented in his own meetings.

I saw that approached and decided I would give it a shot. I went into a session on my own. This was one given by Connie Hamilton and Starr Sackstein, who wrote the book, Hacking Homework. I began taking notes, looking for their video clips and visuals. By the end of the session, I had this document full of notes, ideas, visuals, and videos. Had I just listened, I would've picked up a couple of tidbits here and there, but because I was so engaged, I had really detailed points to bring back to my department. In fact, I based one of my best department meeting sessions off of those notes. More importantly, I came back with detailed research that helped me understand the "why" about my belief that homework was in need of reform. I was a better teacher because I was more engaged in the session.

Since then, I sit in sessions, banging away at the keyboard, filling notes. When I'm in a session with Kris, I try to compete with him to have more notes. I have yet to beat him, but being engaged helps me get more out of a session and helps me retain and better pass along that information.

Opposites Approach: One Strength, One Weakness

Like Mike Trout and other elite athletes, developing isn't just about continuing to develop strengths. Continuing to go to workshops about skills that you are good at is easy. It's enjoyable. You are into it. It does make you better and give you a deeper knowledge. All of that is great. But, that philosophy will also hold you back.

Just like our students, we cannot grow as learners and educators if we do not consciously attack and develop our weaknesses. Each year, I will try to get better at one thing. As with most English Teachers, I would struggle with getting feedback to students in an efficient manner when it came to writing. I would genuinely read their writing thoroughly and dutifully make comments, suggestions, and allow for re-writes. The problem was that it was time-consuming and we would often be onto the next thing before I got work back to them. About five years ago, I made the decision to focus on giving more meaningful feedback in a better, more efficient way.

I sought out workshops centered around that topic. I attended workshops that showed how Google Docs allows for more live, real-time feedback. I completed a webinar about using Goobric, an add on for Google Sheets, that would allow a rubric to embedded into a student's doc and allow for me to give voice recorded feedback as well. When working with Angela Stockman, I focused in on read-behinds, which is looking at student work as they are writing.
With all of that knowledge, my classroom dynamic transformed. Writing conferences became the norm with students bringing me in-progress work and having a discussion about their plan, some suggestions, and some on the fly troubleshooting. The results have been immense in that I am now giving more meaningful feedback to kids as they are working rather than after they have finished.

None of that would be happening had I not specifically attacked a weakness in my skill set. When it comes to professional development, continue to develop a passion by attending at least one workshop on something you are good at or passionate about. But, balance that by attending a professional development session that addresses something you must improve. By taking that balanced approach, you are not only amplifying one of your best assets in the classroom, but you are also developing skills that need that attention and will ultimately make you a more well-rounded teacher for kids.

Read One Book...Read More

I'll be the first one to admit it; I find it difficult to read books about teaching. There's probably some irony in that statement, no?

It's not that I don't think I can learn something. I know I can learn something. But, I like reading for enjoyment. I like reading to escape. But, if I want to evolve as an educator, I must read. I must keep current. I must see what others have to say.

I have developed a system over the past year that has helped me with reading books from the education field. I now have a routine where I will force myself to sit and read for 10 minutes a day. I usually do so before heading off to bed. Most nights that 10 minutes turns out to be at least 30 minutes, sometimes an hour. Developing that routine has helped me read some great books over the past year such as Culturize, The One Thing, Better Than Carrots and Sticks, Fair Is Not Always Equal, and Start With The Why. By committing just 10 minutes a day, I have gained perspectives that allow me to be better in the classroom.

I am better, however, at reading articles, blogs, and listening to podcasts. While I find it much easier to read about baseball, I do make the effort to read at least two professional articles per week. Whether it is subscribing to a blog feed, receiving a newsletter, getting the latest magazine from ACSD, or listening to a podcast on the way into work, there is so much information out there. The beauty is that with all of that information, you can execute the plan of focusing on one strength and one weakness by sifting through publications for pieces that address those topics. Or, you can just read and/or listen to whatever strikes you as interesting. The more you consume, the better you will be in the classroom whether it sparks ideas, gives you a different perspective on kids, or highlights a strategy for you to employ.

Extending the Network: Social Media

I'll be honest: I have been on Twitter since 2007. I didn't start using it as an education tool until 2018. I was definitely late to that game. For me, social media was a connection to all news, especially sports news. I'd follow sportswriters and publications to get news, links to interesting articles and analysis, and have conversations. I dabbled in Facebook a bit for that, but Twitter was more of what I needed. I also used it as a way to develop an audience for my writing. But, education? I never thought it would be useful.

It wasn't until Kris decided to launch a Twitter challenge for our District that I saw the value to education. There are so many talented educators out there who are chatting about education, who are writing about education, and who are collaborating on ideas. Every day, you can find ideas, inspiration, and links to great content through social media. It is like having 24-hour access to professional development with no limits on what you can consume. Through Twitter, I have been exposed to the work of some great education minds by reading their work, listening to some of their talks, and seeing their chats.

We want our students to be lifelong learners and to continually seek out knowledge. Social Media gives educators that opportunity from their phones. Expert advice for immediate use in a classroom is just a tweet away. If we want to teach our students how to use social media responsibly and for good, we must become practitioners. By doing so, we break out of the "close the door" mentality and truly learn the meaning of collaboration, extend our crew beyond our buildings, find more tools to add to our toolboxes, and find more content to continue to develop our strengths while trying to address our weaknesses. That isn't a waste of time; that is caring enough to continue to grow in our profession. By doing so, we are giving the best of us to our students.

Thankfully, the industry's attitudes and, more importantly, its offerings have changed for professional development. We now have every opportunity to get better at our jobs. We now have zero excuses. Surrounded by our crew, our collective attitude towards professional development can be that of wanting to improve and wanting to innovate. With that attitude, that work ethic, and with all of the resources available, we can truly transform our industry that will better prepare kids to change the world.

Professional Development Takeaways for Admins

→ The greatest resource any school has is people; treat them as such.

→ Invest in the health and wellness of your staff; it is worth the time and money in the long run.

→ Focus on your teachers' strengths and build upon them.

→ Be creative when you provide PD to teachers. PowerPoints and sit and get professional development gets old...quick!

→ Offer choice in professional learning opportunities, good teaching and learning do not have to look the same in every classroom.

→ Let people know what to expect, always give the time to review the plan any time you meet with your staff.

→ Set your expectations prior to the start of any session; it is better to remind participants to stay off their tech before you start than to become upset once you have started when heads are buried in phones.

→ Encourage teachers learning from teachers and put systems in place that make it not only possible, but convenient.

→ It is the job of the administrator to inspire lifelong learners; conformity based structures do not lead to authentic learning.

Professional Development Takeaways for Teachers

→ The "one thing" mentality must be used when attending professional development. You will often get much out of sessions, but focus on acquiring one thing to bring back to the classroom.

→ Surround yourself with colleagues who want to talk about education and want to plan.

→ Share your practices, watch others.

→ Professional Development isn't about showing you how to do something. It is to add to your toolbox.

→ Elite athletes and performers are driven to acquire more skills. Elite Teachers are the same.

→ Take detailed notes to stay engaged during PD Sessions.

→ Social Media can be used to connect with educators around the world.

→ Amplify your strengths by attending a session. But, balance that by challenging yourself to improve on a weakness.

→ Commit a small amount of time each day to read something about the field.

VOICES FROM THE FIELD...
Evan Robb, Principal

How am I promoting professional growth? Are adults either learners or not? These are two questions I reflect on frequently. Although I work to create an invitational environment in my school, choosing to grow or not can't be an option. When educators lead by offering invitational growth, those who are excited seek out opportunities to grow and transform. Those who choose not to partake fall further behind. Invitational growth creates a bimodal staff. My affirmation, if my leadership style is too invitational, I give some permission not to change and grow, which is not fair to students.

Recently I was in a meeting discussing professional growth and permission to take risks. I can recall my words, 'Dynamic learner-centered classrooms will always be lead by dynamic teachers. You cannot have an old-fashioned rigid teacher leading a progressive and dynamic classroom. The same parallel is true for a school.'

Progressive schools empower staff and students to take risks and grow as learners and thinkers because these schools, teachers and their principals value: learning, creativity, innovation, taking risks, relationship building, and view making mistakes as information that can support positive change.

But why are some schools and classrooms growth focused while others appear so different? What role can a school leader play in developing a commitment to professional growth? To me, this starts with the principal who must consistently model the expectation of what is important, professional growth. Through actions and beliefs, school leaders can demonstrate how professional growth is important for staff. Leading by example can give teachers permission to take risks and to grow as learners. This can encourage teachers to try something new or seek out information to improve their performance through learning. Article studies, book studies, using a personal learning network, these are just some ways professionals can grow. A mindset committed to professional growth increases teacher agency, personal efficacy and collective efficacy for a school. Schools need engaged teachers who can apply their learning and beliefs in students to improve their teaching, leading to better student outcomes.

The world we are preparing students for is far different than what we experienced in school. And we educators need to prepare our students for this changing world, the uncertainties, and unknowns of the future. Empower and inspire staff to grow as learners and give them permission to try. Lead the change. Collaboratively create a culture celebrating learning, staff and students need and deserve innovative schools committed to professional growth.

5

Homework Done Better

"The most dangerous phrase in the language is, 'we've always done it that way'."
--Grace Hopper

Thus far, we have talked about building a team, communicating with parents, inspiring students, and getting better as professionals. One of the areas of education that has long been neglected is homework. While there is extensive research showing its limited value, and often times detrimental impact on student learning, this area is still stuck in the land of "what we've always done."

When the concept of homework--even the concept of school--was first developed, it was based on the factory model. We needed to produce a workforce that could accomplish rote tasks. Obviously, we are preparing kids for a far different landscape, yet many homework practices are still archaic. Students have evolved and can utilize technology to complete these pedestrian, rote tasks. Or, they spend endless hours fulfilling requirements, rather than truly deepening their learning or enhancing their passions.

The Admin must set a tone of a district, a building that allows for teachers to think differently and truly find ways to inspire learning and develop those important characteristics that we all want for our kids: a problem solver, critical thinker, and someone who continually wants to learn.

The Teacher must truly break away from the long history of homework and flip the mindset to that of home learning where students are given options, home learning is something that is actually needed, not required, and where home learning is student driven. Thankfully, the field is looking at this type of reform.

The Admin

Some memories stay with you long after they should. One such memory for me was my kindergarten screening. Of course, at the time, I didn't know it was called that. All I knew was that my grandmother was bringing me to the place I would have to go for the next thirteen years of my life, which as a four-year old might as well have been an eternity.

What do you mean I will have to sit still all day? What do you mean I will have to listen to my teacher? What do you mean my nan won't be able to read me my favorite stories, play jacks, or crazy 8s with me?

The day was filled with apprehension and defiance. My emotions were high that day, explaining why, over 40 years later, I can still smell the distinct dust smell of the old Milton Elementary School gym.

We pulled away in my nan's white Pinto when she asked, "aren't you excited you get to go to school next year?"

"No, Nan I decided I am not going to go to school. I am going to stay with you."

She chuckled at declaration, but I could also see a small tear well up in her eye. She loved the time we spent together as much as I did. She was my pal. We loved our time together and I couldn't imagine how I would learn more about going to school than from her.

She tried to put my mind at ease by talking about the friends I would make, the field trips I would go on, and the garden show! The garden show was a tradition a Milton Elementary School where the students had to present one of nature's glories to the parents and students. The winner would get a big blue ribbon and, more importantly, their name in Southern Ulster Times. I came close one year when I covered a variety of fruits and vegetables with melted wax from a machine designed to help my mother recover from a foot injury. I cried at my second place finish, but Betsy, the winner, had grown an apple inside a jug for god sake.

I was starting to come around when my grandmother mis-stepped and said, "besides I am sure they won't give you much if any homework in Kindergarten."

Wait, what?

What is this homework you speak of?

So, I have to go to school all day for eight hours. I have to sit still; I'm not allowed to speak unless I am given permission, I am not even allowed to go to the bathroom without permission, and I still have to do more school work when I get home?

When will we get to play? When we will have the chance to go to Lloyds?

"This is a bunch of Baloney!"

I had yet to develop my colorful bag of expletives so baloney was the best I could do at the time.

Little did I know it then, but it started a 40-year hate affair with homework. Each year the workload seemed to increase. Each year the teachers would point out how bad my handwriting was, how sloppy I was, how I was not serious enough as a student. I can still feel the overwhelming restlessness and anger in my stomach when I had to sit down and complete what I thought were dumb and useless assignments. Looking back I was right in most cases; they were dumb, they were useless. What in the world did it teach me to hunt and peck my way through my Social Studies textbook and regurgitate the answers in complete sentences?

It did not help my learning or attitude when I was chastised for incomplete, sloppy work. It actually contributed to the exact opposite. I was seen for so long by many teachers as someone who was more interested in sports, girls, and getting a good laugh.

I was not seen as a writer because my handwriting was poor and that my grammar and spelling was atrocious.

I was not seen as a hard worker because my work was often turned in late or done poorly.

I was not seen as a serious student because I was often fidgeting in my seat, asking to go to the bathroom, or disrupting the class.

It is ironic that today I have to be reminded to slow down, to avoid taking on more work, to leave my job at the office so I can give my family the attention they deserve.

When I speak about homework reform and retell the stories of me copying homework on the bus from the "smart kids" or how my mother would often do my homework for me, I get looks. I am not sure if they are looks of disgust that one of the leaders of our district talks so openly about cheating, or if they do not believe that someone who often works 60 hour works weeks actually didn't do his homework.

When we are told that homework builds responsibility, builds character, builds work ethic, I disagree. Maybe the right homework can help to accomplish these goals, but certainly not the rote tasks I was asked to do as a child. Sadly, these are assignments, that in many schools, have not changed all that much.

Many adults are hardworking, responsible, driven people not because of all the life lessons that homework taught them. I suspect, in fact, that many successful adults had to overcome preconceived notions that they were lazy, ordinary, or disorganized because they hated homework as much as I did.

It is amazing how we can be so penny wise and dollar foolish in the field of education. We spend thousands of dollars to educate each child each year. We are the lifeline for students who are facing impossible home situations. We try to make the most of our limited time with students, teaching a massive and, many times, meaningless curriculum and yet we waste our energy, our minutes, making students who do not complete homework feel as if they are lazy, inadequate, or unintelligent. What employee would be able to be their best if upon arrival to work each day the boss pointed out what they had not accomplished, not at work, but during their own free time?

It seems silly to me and, fortunately, many educators I know are trying to make changes in how homework is assigned, assessed, and used to support learning.

The first step in true homework reform is honest and open discussion. We must as important questions such as:

? Why do we give homework?

? How does homework support the goals and objectives of our lessons?

? Is homework a fair assessment if we cannot be sure if the student completed it on their own?

? If homework was optional, would it become less or more authentic?

? How can homework be better designed to align with what students need?

? How can learning beyond the school day become about authentic learning rather than compliance?

? How can we truly teach students to be responsible?

? How do we get students to think and reflect on their learning, rather than completing a task for a grade?

The more I research homework, the more I read about homework, the more I speak to students, teachers, and parents, the more I am convinced that homework in its current state is a product of "the way we have always done it" way of thinking.

There is certainly a place for expanding the learning beyond the school day, but, in its current form, homework is hurting education more than it is helping. We can do better and must do better.

I have seen some excellent approaches to thinking about homework differently. Based on these observations I have started to formulate a list of non-negotiables for homework design:

Homework Design

- The purpose of the assignment and how it supports their learning must be clear to students.

- Feedback must be provided. It is unfair to ask students to spend their youth completing assignment after assignment and receive a check for completion the next day.

- Homework should count minimally or not at all in a child's grade.

- Homework should not cost families money to complete.

- Although homework can be used to build background knowledge, it should never be used to "cover things we didn't get to"

- Students should not be disciplined or scolded for not completing homework. We get precious little time with them in the classroom. We should never waste it by damaging their desire to learn.

In my District, I have tackled this controversial topic. This three-year battle is coming to an end and I am confident that we will be making real changes in practice and policy that will benefit my District long after I leave.

One of the unintended consequences of this journey has been the schooling I have received from the teachers in my District. I have changed my opinions and preconceived notions. I have had some first-rate educational discussions and I have acquired ideas for how homework can be done better.

Ideas for Homework Done Different

Performance-Based

A first-year band teacher recently explained that he uses different color strings that serve as "Karate Belts." When students are able to demonstrate competency in their playing abilities, they are awarded a different belt. Play Hot Cross Buns get a yellow, Star Wars, a theme purple, etc... Kevin explained that this strategy has students visiting his room during lunch to practice and more than one student has gotten into some hot water by practicing in the hallway, on the bus, or in the cafeteria.

Question boards

This is a place, either electronic or physical, where the teacher poses a question on the lesson and students react and respond.

? What is something that you need more help with?

? What do you think was the most important part of today's lesson?

? What do you think motivated explorers to sail the seas?

? Why have we not discovered life in the universe?

? Do you think we someday will?

? How can you use what you have learned this week in your life?

Read

The best home learning assignment in my mind is still reading, and reading without logs, without question, without anything. Just teaching kids how to find a book they love and giving them the opportunity to find joy in one of life's greatest pleasures.

Providing Students with a Guide

The teacher explains all of the competencies that are needed for an upcoming assessment and provides them with various activities that can help them to gain the knowledge they need. Khan Academy videos, YouTube videos, practice problems, readings, teacher-designed videos, notes, audio files, student discussions, the list goes on and on and gets bigger each day as technology becomes easier to use and more accessible.

Parent Support Activities

One of the biggest gripes parents have especially at the elementary level when homework is not assigned is that they do not know what's going on in the classroom. Progressive teachers are providing parents with weekly or bi-weekly reports that look something like this:

Subject	ELA	Math	SS	Science	Character
Key concepts taught in class					
Questions to ask your child					
Practice activities to reinforce classroom learning					
Enrichment activities					
What's next					

Genius Hour

If it is good enough for Google, why not as a way to expand learning beyond the schoolhouse? Giving students permission to explore and learn about topics that they are passionate about can yield incredible results. Teachers who try this may find strengths that they never knew their students had.

Observations

Kids and adults miss so much in today's busy world that is right in front of their eyes. Ask students to observe, look for connections, develop a hypothesis. How many different types of trees are growing in your neighborhood? What do you notice about how they grow? What would your neighborhood be like without trees? You can build similar strands of questions on a variety of subjects, including buildings, cities, waterflow, traffic, the nighttime sky, their mood, their energy level, and so on.

Encouraging observations about the world they live in will not only make concepts you are teaching more real, you are also teaching students to be more present and naturally curious of the world they live in. This is a gift they can carry throughout their lives, unlike the packets that get tossed in the circular file each time they clean out lockers.

Interactions

It is our job to teach our students how to be good people, people who can successfully interact with others. Yet, how much time is spent discussing how to talk to people? Respectful conversations, eye contact, not taking out your phone when you are speaking to someone? I was shocked last year when one of my leadership council students explained that they were never taught how to write an email and his generation really didn't "get" email much like I don't "get" snapchat.

How valuable would it have been had my son been asked to discuss what it was like to flee Nazi Germany with his grandparents and great uncles at the Bat Mitzvah we attended rather than the stress-inducing assignment we completed at 1:00 AM? Students can be taught how to initiate these conversations, brainstorm respectful questions to ask, then have them for discussion in class. This seems to be a much more authentic way to explore enduring questions than traditional means. Our families have rich stories to tell and lessons to teach, but it does not have to stop there. Emails, letters, questions, real-life exploration, and research may not be as easy to quantify as a worksheet, but they certainly offer skills and knowledge that will endure much longer.

Involve Students

A conversation with a veteran teacher served as an epiphany for me. We were on different sides of the homework debate in a lot of ways, but his approach to homework was one I could not deny was brilliant. He designed the homework with his students, not for his students. He explained to his students what they need to accomplish and then asked the students to determine what assignments would best help them to reach his classroom goals.

I wondered how he had time to meet with all of his students individually like this, and questioned if they would even know where to begin.

"It's a learning process. I spend some whole group time teaching them what are some options and, earlier in the year, I have to spend more time with them individually. But, after they have been taught how they can best support their learning, it becomes almost second nature and some of it the communication can be done through Google Classroom."

He went on to describe how these individual conversations were where some of his best teaching and connecting happened. He also mentioned that meeting with students universally provided his students with time to read, something he had been wanting to incorporate in his class for years. This teacher counts homework much more than I would or that I think is appropriate (15%), but it is hard to dispute that his approach helps to develop responsibility, student efficacy, and better prepare students when they leave the nest and head off to college or career.

Kids may no longer be copying homework on the bus or in homeroom. In fact, it has gotten easier to 'game" homework. They now have group chats, Photomath, Socratic, and pay for homework sites like "Do My Homework"

We must realize that we cannot make kids or anyone for that matter do anything they do not want to do. Educators can drive themselves to the brink trying to ensure students learn the way they are supposed to learn. At the end of the day, isn't it more important that they do, in fact, learn? Wouldn't our time and energy be better spent than dishing out consequences to students when they do not do their homework?

We can guide them, show them how to support their own learning. We can expose them to new ways to learn; we can provide them with the opportunity to explore, to have a different relationship with work after the school day ends.

When homework stops being about grades, about conformity, about what I say you must do, then we are teaching our kids responsibility, getting them ready for college, and maybe, just maybe, keep them as excited and motivated when they are in High School as they were in Kindergarten.

The Teacher

I had a conversation with a parent recently that best summed up my feelings about homework and how it can be done so much better for kids. I had bumped into this parent in the hallway and mentioned that her daughter did so well on a group project that required extensive research, an individual 1,200-word paper, and that group presentation that had to be eight to ten minutes long.

"Karly really nailed the presentation. She was so good. She was confident, spoke so powerfully, and was even referring to charts in the presentation."

"She really practiced. She spoke in front of a mirror. She practiced in front of us. The kids face-timed a lot to practice. And, they went over each other's houses on the weekends a few times," said her Mom, who also was a teacher.

"Really? That's incredible. You could tell that they had it all together. They practiced a ton in class and were constantly rewriting their papers too."

"They were so into their topic. You have to know that they love your class, right?"

And, with that, we finished up the conversation, but I walked away smiling. Kids never really get credit for all of their hard work and dedication. Kids never get credit for their thoroughness, their care, or their desire to do their best. They never get credit for their preparation. Because of that lack of credit, the education industry feels the need to give more work in order to develop those qualities. This often comes in the form of homework.

Let's get one thing straight: Kids need to work hard. They need to show dedication. They need to be thorough so they can master problems and skills. They need to show that they are doing their best at all times. They need to prepare for the rigors of life.

Many teachers believe that homework is a way to develop all of those things.

Many teachers are wrong.

Or, at the very least, they are misguided in how they are assigning that work.

Here's the thing---that dedicated young lady and her group of friends who spent time on the weekends and during the weeknights doing their work?

They chose to do that.

It wasn't homework. I don't assign homework; I haven't assigned homework in years. Yet, there was a group of teenagers who chose to do their very best, even after I gave them all of our class time to complete the project. That's probably the key part of this story. Their class time was spent working on this project with me in there as a guide. They didn't procrastinate or waste time in class. They worked each day and would've done a fine job with the final products had they just used the time in class. But, they wanted to do more; they wanted better.

And, that group certainly wasn't alone. The other groups in the class put in a similar amount of effort. That really wasn't all that surprising to me since I had lived through this course just a year before. My previous group of students was so into the projects that I once had to send a message through our Google Classroom that they needed to go to bed, rather than continue to stay up perfecting their papers and working on their presentations.

Often, I receive emails after 10:00 PM from students asking me to help them revise their paper. Because I don't sleep, I will often "hop on" their doc and go through some revisions with them. To me, it is gratifying because my students could be doing other things, yet they care enough about their writing to continue to work at it in their free time.

Because of my experiences with students, I firmly believe that the education system would be better without homework. If we completely cut it out tomorrow, kids would still learn and would still be productive. They do not need these ancient, rote tasks to complete in order to continue to develop as learners. But, I realize that we are fighting a century's worth of practices and beliefs here. We are fighting myth, fueled by tradition.

Blasting Through the Myths

Myth #1: Homework Prepares for College Responsibilities
One of the expressions that should be driven out of secondary education is "this will prepare you for college." While we are at it, let's eliminate that "next level" expression from the middle and primary levels too. Education, at all levels, isn't about prepping for the next level. It isn't about preparing a student just for those four years of college. The education system should be preparing students to succeed in any life situation, not just for college. If a school system is doing right by kids, those kids will graduate ready to succeed in any area, not just college.

But, let's entertain the notion of preparing a student for college. Homework supporters like to say that homework prepares students for the grind of college. Kids have to be able to have the capacity to do work on their own. They have to develop the responsibility to work on their own and manage their time. Thus, assigning a couple of hours of work each night for a student is under the guise of preparing.

It's false logic.

College programs don't work like that. Professors hand out a syllabus with the work for the semester listed. Thus, a student has to manage his/her time and stay organized, two big traits that fall under the definition of responsibility. Students are assigned reading and generally given multiple days to complete, rather than for the next day. They are not asked to complete graphic organizers, submit their answers to basic questions, or complete dittos. They are asked to manage their time, schedule work and study time, and manage multiple long term deadlines. Those are skills that develop responsibility.

Yet, that is the exact opposite of what most homework looks like in schools today. The models of schools and colleges are completely different. Homework every night isn't teaching the traits needed to be a responsible college student.

I can vividly remember one time when I had a student come into my class looking particularly exhausted. I asked her if she was ok. She said that she was tired because she had so much homework. It turned out that she got home around 5:30 PM from swimming practice. After a quick shower and grabbing some food to eat in her room, she got moving on her homework. It took her about 90 minutes to complete her math. Then she moved onto to science. When the clock hit 11:00 PM, she decided that she needed sleep. Her alarm went off at 2:00 AM so she could finish her Social Studies. That doesn't sound much like a college prep program. That generally isn't how life works either.

Some may call that being a responsible student. Instead, it is something far from the concept of responsibility.

Myth #2: Homework Prepares for Life Responsibilities

There is the myth that homework prepares students for their life responsibilities. After all, when they are in the workforce, they will put in days of eight, ten, or maybe even twelve hours. Then, they'll have to go home every night and work for another couple of hours on additional work that is due the next day. Isn't that how every job works?

Of course, it doesn't. Most jobs—even teaching jobs—allow people to have lives outside of work. Some jobs may require extra, long hours. And, some jobs may require that you bring home work once in a while. But, no job or lifestyle requires you to do two to three extra hours of work after putting in a full day, every single day. Most jobs allow for other interests like hobbies and even time with family.

One day, when my daughter was in fourth grade, she came home from school with more homework than usual. There were 20 math problems that each required two different ways of solving. There was a literary response sheet, a vocabulary exercise that required 20 words used in sentences, and the 20 minutes of reading. Add to this, it was kickboxing night, an activity she loved. Honestly, I saw it and knew all of it couldn't get done along with dinner, a bath, and a reasonable bedtime. I told her I would write a note saying that we couldn't get it all done and that I made the decision to not complete everything.

But, my daughter loved her teacher and that love was justified. Her teacher is the best I've seen. She was nervous about letting her down. Ultimately, she chose to skip kickboxing. It was one of those parent moments where I didn't know what to do. As a teacher, I don't believe in homework, but here is my kid actually upset that she couldn't complete it. After realizing that she would be more anxious if she didn't complete her homework, we stayed home and labored through it all.

To her teacher's credit–and proof that she is, indeed, the best–when we spoke to her at conferences about this particular night, she brought my daughter in the room and said, "You never skip kickboxing again. You need to do the things you love. Never worry about homework."

Some may look at my daughter and say that she has her priorities in line at a young age and made a mature decision to be responsible and do her homework. Instead, it is something far from the concept of responsibility.

Myth #3: Homework Completion Proves a Student is Responsible
Both of those stories lead us to the final myth. The way that the majority of the education industry does homework does not foster responsibility. My student wasn't showing responsibility by forgoing sleep. My daughter wasn't showing responsibility by skipping kickboxing. Both were exhibiting compliance.

Most mistake responsibility for compliance. Responsibility is about being able to act independently and make decisions. Compliance is about obeying a command to simply meet some given standard.

Which word sounds more like a description of how homework is done in schools?

If we want to foster the concept of responsibility in schools, why are we using a system that really is about compliance?

Do this homework tonight or your grade will suffer.

Complete this ditto or fill out this graphic organizer so I have proof you did something.

Complete these 20 math problems because showing me you could do four wasn't enough.

Are any of those examples of responsibility?

All this does is set up a system where students look for ways to "get it done", rather than focus on learning.

Myth 4: Homework is a Sign of Rigor

The word rigor is one of the most misused, misinterpreted words in the education field. Most often, it is synonymous with the concept of more or even difficult. But, that isn't what rigor means. Instead, rigor means challenging. And, that is a concept that should be discussed more in education.

All people need to be challenged. Our thinking needs to be challenged. It is our job as Teachers to challenge our students. Challenging doesn't mean silent classrooms. Challenging doesn't mean piling on worksheet after worksheet. And, challenging certainly doesn't mean giving homework nightly.

Challenging means inspiring students to think, not comply. Challenging them means inspiring them to find something they are passionate about and to want to seek more. Challenging them means to help them create a balance.

Homework, sadly, is used with the misguided definition of the word, rigor: a lot of it is given, almost none of it is inspiring. In fifth grade, my daughter has the same homework each night: a math ditto, a reading ditto, and a handwriting ditto. There is nothing else. 180 days of school equals about 600 dittos. Not surprisingly, a kid who loves to read and write and actually wants to learn isn't inspired and often asks to stay home. The love of learning has been extinguished a bit. That inspiration her fourth grade teacher would give with research topics and menu choices for reading that resulted in "I can't miss a day of Mrs. Heraghty's class" is now an "I can't wait for fifth grade to be over." Compliance in the name of rigor squashes the one thing we should be fostering in all kids of all ages: a love of learning.

Rigor is not endless chapter outlines, so many annotations that a text is covered in post its, hours of math work to master a concept, and outdated, outmoded worksheets that do little else than force basic recall. Rigor is not about taking up a students' time or making them give up activities or sleep in order to "prove" that they belong in a class.

Reframing Homework

While I am an extremist, I realize that homework can be something that extends passions if done correctly. I do see my students want to work at home because they want to do better. They want to revise their writing. They want to work on their presentations. They want to read a book that they are caught up in.

Now, some may look at my current teaching load and see advanced placement classes. Yes, those students are motivated. But, in my two decades in a classroom, I have only taught that level for two years. I can remember teaching our PM School program, which was an alternative program for students who did not thrive in the traditional classroom. They would come to school at 3:00 PM and have classes until after 7:00 PM. Many of these students were not fans of school. Obviously, they were there for a reason.

But, I still tell my current students' stories about that group and their dedication. These were students who were removed from the traditional setting, yet they came to my class with a passion because they had a voice in their learning.

When it was time to read a novel, I would go into our book room and grab every grade level title we had. I'd lay them out and give a quick talk about them. Then, I would have them pick the ones they wanted to read. They would form book groups. I'd give them time in class to read and told them that they could take their time reading them. We'd do book talks twice a week where they would group up with students with the same book.

I would always be in my room early, waiting for them to arrive. One day, a young man came in early. He sat there with his book. He was thumbing through To Kill A Mockingbird. I was surprised that few kids picked that book, but four of them did.

"Hey, how do you like the book so far?"

"I finished it last night, Armida."

"I just gave it to you two days ago. What made you finish it so quick?"

"I don't know; I just got into it. But, I have to tell you, I think Atticus is a punk."

"Really?"

"Yeah, his daughter is fooled thinking he is perfect and all that."

"Why?"

"It's not like he wanted to be that guy's lawyer. The judge made him."

And, we kept talking for another 20 minutes, even as the rest of the class filed in. He mentioned the trial and how he felt Atticus didn't fight hard enough and how he would've done things differently with Mayella (or, "that white girl" as he said).
He read the book, not because I forced him to. He read the book because he chose to. He was inspired by the words. He liked the subject. He gave up two nights to read the book.

It doesn't matter what level a student is on. All students—all people—want to be challenged. We all want rigor. But, we want a real challenge, something that makes us think. It has to be something we are inspired by.

So, how can we do homework better?

First, we must be confident enough in our own instruction to realize that we don't have to give students rote tasks in order to validate that we did something with them. All that does is create an environment with little thinking and, more dangerously, little passion.

Second, we must shift our mindset from the idea of homework to home learning. While that sounds like semantics, the shift is important. Work is about the factory model; it is about compliance. Learning is about deepening and enhancing skills. It is about finding a passion, cultivating that passion, and producing something important.

Home Learning is Options & Skills

Teaching is about helping kids to develop skills. Our content is the vehicle to unlock and develop those talents. Therefore, students should be given plenty of options on how to demonstrate their skills. As an English Teacher, this can be easily done.

We have kids read books for a number of reasons. Obviously, we want them to make connections to themselves and the world. Writers write for a reason and we want kids to develop the skills to discover those reasons. We also want to use literature as an example for writing instruction. And, of course, there are the standards. Students should be able to identify how literary devices are used and why they are used (among many standards). This can be done with a variety of literature.

Why are we beholden to teaching one particular novel when we know that we will lose some kids due to a lack of interest? As adults, we pick and choose literature based on our interest. We don't allow students that choice. And, when kids aren't interested, they either don't read it or go find the 2019 version of Cliff Notes.

A common complaint made by teachers and parents is that kids don't read.

Reworded: kids don't read what we want them to read.

Kids, regardless of their academic level, will read if they are interested. One of my favorite ways to get kids to read outside of class is to use Literature Circles.

Literature Circles are book groups where kids form their own groups, choose a group book based on their interest, assign their own reading to be done, assign jobs for them to complete when doing their independent reading, and then meet together to discuss the reading. After the discussion meeting, they assign additional reading and jobs. The process repeats until it is done.

Book choice can be done a couple of different ways. I've had groups go to the library and pick out any book. Or, as I did with my PM School class, I pick out a bunch of texts from the curriculum. If a group has a different idea, they can pitch the idea. Why should it matter if all groups are reading different books? If it is about skills, the text is irrelevant. And, if they chose something, they are more invested. If they are more invested, they are far more likely to read.

What am I doing in between meetings? If we are learning skills related to reading, we are either looking at excerpts from different works, using a short story or poem, or even a selection from a group's book to learn the skills as a class. Or, we are applying those skills in our writing. In other words, they are practicing their skills with me. Hopefully, by giving them a choice of what to read, they will develop a passion for reading or the subject matter. And, they'll actually want to work at home because they are invested.

And, that AP Class project from the beginning of this chapter? Well, all of the topics were chosen by the students. I was still able to teach skills and concepts. But, their product and the work they ultimately chose to do at home was based on their choice and interests.

Home Learning is a Chance to Go Deeper

If we want to inspire kids, our work in the class should make them want to learn more. When students are genuinely interested in something, they make the time to experience more. I've seen this in my classroom with writing. Our writing journals are a place where we do creative writing exercises, work on different types of writing techniques, etc. Often, we'll use a scenario for a story so that they can work on a specific skill. Our 42-minute sessions are usually not enough for students to write a complete story. But, that's not really the point of these exercises. So many kids, however, go home and finish them. They may not do it that night or even that week, but inevitably I get, "Hey, Armida, read this." That's awesome.

This also extends into every subject. I had experienced that with my daughter and her great fourth grade teacher. Her teacher told us on "Meet the Teacher Night" that she had a passion for social studies and couldn't wait to get to their big project. When they got to the Revolutionary War research project that culminated in a "live" wax museum presentation (during school hours), my daughter was excited. She was allowed to pick her own person and find any sort of materials. The research, documentation, and much of the project was done in class. In other words, all of the skills were being learned in this fourth grade classroom.

Because my daughter had a choice, she's really interested in this project. She chose Major Andre, who, evidently, was a British spy and was hanged for his crimes. I mentioned to her that a restaurant not too far from us was where he was kept during the trial. She wanted to go and take pictures. On her February vacation, she chose to go to this place, which also led to going to a nearby museum where George Washington stayed and then the actual hanging site. This wasn't required, but she went deeper because she had a choice and was given the opportunity. Kids will want to do more if they are interested.

Home Learning is About the Process, Not the Grade

If homework is truly about deepening understanding, allowing for students to experience the curriculum, and is something valuable to the learning experience, why should students be graded? Why is perfection expected in the process of learning?

Most educators will agree that homework is not a valid assessment as there are many factors out of the Teacher's control—parental involvement, student access to technology, student home responsibilities, poverty, etc. If that's the case, why the grade?

It then becomes punitive. Once that happens, it is no longer about learning; it is simply about keeping a kid busy and in check.

Rigor involves being thorough and going beyond the expectation. Grading homework does the opposite. It discourages deeper thought and students being willing to be creative.

Of course, the classic argument will come up stating that students won't complete the homework if it isn't graded. Well, there are a couple of simple responses. First, if students are inspired and have ownership of their learning, they will complete. And, two, the students who don't complete it weren't likely to complete it if it were graded.

Home Learning is Student Driven

The world has changed. The idea of traditional homework has to change. If Home Learning is student-driven, it will be about developing individual strengths, addressing individual challenges, and achieving that romantic notion of producing life-long learners.

Homework, in its traditional sense, is an obstacle to developing creative thinkers and problem solvers. We must evolve.

Kids are already evolving. They are already disproving the notion that they are not aware and that they do not care. This generation has a far greater capacity to learn and think than they've ever been given credit for. They've shown that in some of the most real-world situations that our generation has failed to address. Changing our attitudes and practices about home learning will not only create more intellectually curious people, but it will also make for more creative, engaging classrooms. We can give them choice, options, and more creative materials to work with. Our industry can and must evolve to cultivate kids' strengths and passions.

We owe it to them.

Home Learning Takeaways for Admins

→   The purpose of each home learning activity should be clear to students.

→   Feedback should always be provided in a timely and productive manner.

→   If the true purpose of work beyond the school day is to support the learning that goes on in the classroom, it does not make sense to penalize students who demonstrate understanding on the assessments.

→   Never penalize a student for something their parents didn't do. Signing tests, bringing tissues, or filling out paperwork are often beyond a child's control. If they have inadequate parents they are already at a disadvantage; do not add to that.

→   Reading is the best home learning activity you can assign, but please no reading logs!

→   Homework does not teach responsibility, it teaches conformity.

→   Provide students with options on how they can deepen their understanding of the standards they will be assessed on. When they take ownership of their learning they are demonstrating responsibility.

→   Ask students to think, talk, ask, create, rather than assigning tasks that "Alexa" can complete for them.

→   Students are more than just students, keep this in mind and refrain from homework on weekends and breaks.

Home Learning Takeaways for Teachers

→   Rote tasks, answers that can be searched up with apps or online are not valuable to student learning and add nothing to your class.

→   Homework completion does not prove that a student is responsible.

→   Homework completion does not prove that a student learned.

→   Assigning homework does not mean that a teacher is rigorous.

→   Giving options for home learning will not only deepen student learning, but ignite passions.

→   Home learning should never be grading. It is about continuing the process of learning.

→   Home learning should always be given feedback.

→   Students will want to go deeper if they are given choice about their work.

VOICES FROM THE FIELD...

Richard W. Allen, Ed.S., Principal (Retired), Adjunct Professor, DisruptED TV Co-Founder/Executive Director, Educational Consultant

Homework is an institution in today's schools and the catalyst for endless debate. There is a clearly marked divide between those who see it as an extension of the day's lesson and a non-negotiable, and the camp of practitioners who see homework as a compliance measure to justify a written or de facto district mandate.

When pressed to justify the assignment of homework, educators, few in number, can point to research that supports their claim.

If instructional practices are to be rooted in research-based findings, then one would be hard-pressed to ignore the work of John Hattie and his exhaustive work studying the mitigating factors leading to student achievement. His meta-analysis examined the impact of homework on student achievement. While the evidence from Hattie's study is clear, it has not deterred many from taking his work out of context to suit a personal or professional narrative.

Like so many institutionalized practices, including high stakes assessments, class rankings, and students sitting in rows, the process of homework has its challenges outside the classrooms. The camps here are fractured as well; the reasons are all too well known and need no mention at the risk of being consumed in the obvious.

So as the debate rages, educators continue their homework practices at the expense of the students' well-being, and the frustration of the parents/guardians who may or may not supervise the "at home" process, let alone know precisely their role in the process or how to help.

It is my hope that the work of Kris Felicello and Gary Armida will finally create clarity and direction to this age-old debate, and provide a useful and fluent set of practices and protocols to make homework what it was always intended to be; meaningful and relevant.

6

Grading Reform

"The successful man will profit from his mistakes and try again in a different way." ~ Dale Carnegie

While homework is certainly an area that we must reform, the larger issue really centers around grades. Grades have been used in an attempt to quantify a students' performance or progress. Whether it is a number or letter system, educators have long struggled with giving accurate grades that are truly reflective of a student's progress.

The problem is that a number clearly does not define learning. A number, at best, represents a snapshot of how a student performed during a singular moment in time. But, we know that learning is never linear. We know that true learning--true mastery--takes moments of failure, moments of relearning, moments of adjustment, and moments of reflection. And, we know that there is never truly an end.

As educators, we must look to do with grades what we are trying to accomplish with homework: we must take on the institution of tradition.

Administrators must create an environment where teachers can place the spotlight back on that process of learning. Yes, admins have to worry about district performance on state assessments and other standardized measures, but if they create a culture where the number isn't the focus, students will genuinely learn and perform well in every area, including those standardized assessments.

Teachers must not be beholden to the tradition of the number. The chase for the number is not the most important thing going on in class. It is learning. Teachers must show students that they are more than a number, that learning is difficult, but well worth the effort. Teachers must genuinely value that process of learning and communicate that to students every day.

The Admin

Do we have it all wrong when it comes to grading in our schools?

We talk about teaching students about responsibility, insisting they take responsibility, lament that kids today are not responsible like kids of yesteryear. Yet, when students are asked to follow a script, to conform, to do it because of the "I say so" mentality, responsibility is not actually being taught, conformity is.

Responsibility is about making decisions, taking ownership in your learning, and prioritizing how your time is spent.

We expect students to do as they are told and when they don't, we consequence them.

Tragically it not always detention or suspension, sometimes it is worse; sometimes students are consequenced through their grades.

That is why I wonder if we have it all wrong. Research supports a growth mindset. The field of education has wholeheartedly embraced the philosophy, yet our grading system pretty much supports the exact opposite.

Unfortunately, too often it is less about obtaining knowledge, skill, or competency and more about "how" and "when" you meet those desired outcomes. Students who do not follow the prescribed path can be perceived as lazy, irresponsible, aloof, and sometimes even fraudulent; they are penalized with a grade that is not based on what they can do or what they know, but whether or not they used the process the school deemed acceptable.

Why does it matter so much how students perform at arbitrary checkpoints? Why does the score on a test mean more than true, practical, and lasting learning?

As a former coach, I find it easy to make connections between education and sport, probably because I know that when kids are motivated by passion, when the rules are fair, when it is clear what the goal is, kids will exceed expectations.

I have found the most unruly students, the ones who are usually unsuccessful at the game of school, turn into the people that I would most trust in the foxhole of life, a fact that can manifest through sport. It is my wish that we can draw these qualities out in the classroom and not just the ball field.

Athletes are not judged on how well they "used to" perform. The most playing time is not given to the athletes who logged the most hours practicing (although practice certainly helps). At the end of the day, athletes are judged on whether or not they help the team win.

School is much different. Grading is used to judge, categorize, rank, and, in the worst cases, consequence students. Why do we hear statements such as, "It is not fair to the kids who handed it on time if I let you redo it" or "If you work really hard and do well on the next test you can make up for the one you bombed during the last unit."

Educators are challenged with teaching in a system that rewards competency on a given assessment, at a random point in time. Is it any wonder that the first question that students ask is "does this count?" A statement that can make even the most poised educator's blood boil.

Educators are frustrated; it seems that parents and students only care about grades, about making the honor roll, about what a score does to their GPA.

They are frustrated by the fact that motivation comes from a number rather than the love of learning. They are frustrated that is rare to find kids who share their passion for the subject they chose to spend their lives teaching.

One of the biggest challenges I faced as a building principal was when quarterly report cards came out. Inevitable calls would be fielded, ones in which parents would complain about teachers or grading practice. Usually, the grievances were more about those few points that prevented their child from receiving academic accolades such as the honor roll, than learning and instruction.

My teachers and I would commiserate and complain about how short-sighted it was for parents to be focused on grades rather than learning. We asked why aren't they supporting us? We were working hard to develop their children into responsible human beings. It was frustrating when it seemed that they only cared about what grade "we gave them"

What I found even more frustrating was when teachers would use the equally detrimental phrase, "I didn't give you that grade, it is what you earned."

It needs to be more about learning than grades! Yet, we have all become so conditioned with the game of grades that we play it and reward those who play it well.

Is it any wonder parents and students prioritize grades, points, and less about how much is learned? That is exactly what our education system values, what college admission officers value.

Grades matter...

Until they don't.

Many educators worry about getting their kids "ready" for Middle School, High School, College, but once those milestones are complete life looks strikingly different than it did during formal schooling.

This is a troubling disconnect. Once our kids enter the world of adulthood, grades become irrelevant. It becomes about performance, collaboration, connections, and skills.

It is rare for an employer to hire based on GPA. In fact, many companies are putting less and less stock into where a prospective employee went to college and in some cases don't if care if they went to college at all.

Grades are destroying the love of learning. In essence, what we have is a rewards-based system that celebrates those willing and able to play the game. It becomes harder and harder to find authentic learning experiences, ones that are intrinsically motivated.

In his 2009 book Drive, Daniel Pink argues that rewards systems work only when people are asked to complete duties with "a defined set of steps, and a single answer." "When we want people to think, create and complete higher level tasks rewards such as monetary bonus actually hurt performance." Pink bases his hypothesis on studies conducted at MIT and other Universities.

Pink also claims that if companies truly want to motivate their workers to perform better they should support "internal drives by providing them with the opportunity to be self-directed, have a purpose for a greater good, and mastery of a particular skill. "

Unfortunately, businesses are slow to make this change, one can hardly blame them, this model worked for so long. The problem is that it no longer does. Our society needs a workforce that can think, be creative. It demands specialization and individualization. Their stale carrots no longer work. Look at the demise of the car industry in Detroit, the bankruptcy of long-standing staples such as Sears, JCPenney, Blockbuster. The list goes on and on.

Our most progressive companies understand this and have flourished; Google, Yahoo, Dropbox, and even municipalities have adjusted.

The city of Houston (Ranked 2nd in FORBES 500 company headquarters), one of our country's fastest growing and most prosperous cities, values people, creativity, and resilience that has been fortified by not only surviving natural disasters like Hurricane Harvey, but thriving and always looking for opportunities to grow.

The business model of rewards and bonuses worked when our country needed factory workers. This is no longer our reality. Businesses will either adapt or fold; it is that simple. It may take some longer than others, but, eventually, those that do not change will drown in the past.

This is what worries me about schools, which are notoriously slow to change, much slower in fact than in the business world where success is easily measured by profit margins.

In schools, it is not as easy to measure success, sparks that are lit in schools do not burst into promise and product until much later.

This does not stop lawmakers from trying to measure the immeasurable. They put a quantifiable value on students, teachers, and schools, using a measure that is outdated, unreliable, or unfair. It doesn't matter if it is a GPA, SAT scores, growth score for a teacher or a ESSA distinction for a school. It is basically a desire to quantify what is often next to impossible to quantify.

I can go into a classroom for 5 minutes and tell if kids feel loved, if the teacher is having a good day or bad day, if learning is happening, if it is a classroom I would want my own child in. It doesn't take an administrative degree or a doctorate; in fact, most educators would be able to walk into the room and tell you the same. I do not need a State test to tell me the value of my teachers. I do not need a 20-page rubric that tries to capture and judge every "best practice" that has ever been invented. I need to see them teach, I need to see them interact with kids, I need to be around them to tell if they add value to our school.

How do you "grade" this? How do you measure this? Those are the questions I wish I had the answer to, but I know as an administrator I need to value those unmeasurable traits that the educational artists demonstrate in their classroom day in and day out.

I know I cannot box my teachers into one way of teaching. I know I have to value the strengths that each of them brings to our profession. I know I need to be courageous enough not to allow an assessment that was created because it was easy to administer and analyze to drive my decisions, put a value on my teachers, predict my students' future based on it.

I know I need to find out what value those that work in our schools bring and not only allow them to run with it but encourage it. What makes each teacher special? What gets them excited to come to work? Administrators need to find that, cultivate that, give their teachers the autonomy to be an artist in the classroom.

When this happens, teachers will be more inclined to do the same for their students. They will begin to see students for what they can do rather than what they can't.

Like the evaluation system for teachers, the grading system for students is archaic; it measures competencies that do not necessarily translate to success in life.

One of education's favorite phrases is to get students "college and career ready." It may be that as I get older I become more jaded, but, in the past, I saw more value in our measures, pushed students to reach for what we deemed a success, but now I am starting to think we have it all wrong.

We may be getting them ready for college, or more accurately to get into college, to help colleges rank them, but we are not getting them as ready for life as we could and should.

Yes, we all need basic competencies, general knowledge, common understandings, but does every child need to master complex math or physics problems? Does every child need to analyze and pick apart Shakespeare? I know classic stories are timeless, but many kids must find it as boring as I do.

Our grading system may have worked in the past, but it is time to evoke change, time to update how we grade to reflect our changing world. What if we were to overcome our fear and put Pink's suggestions into place in our schools? Let's give kids autonomy, give them a cause, allow them to master skills where they show competency and desire.

THE **TEACHER** & THE **ADMIN**

What if we embraced teachers who did things differently and stopped asking them to all be the same, and stopped measuring them the same way?

The education system as designed, rewards mediocrity, jack of all trades, generalists, in a world no longer needs those types of citizens. Robots now complete as Pink says "a defined set of steps, and a single answer."

We need specialists, and creators, artists, and moralists. The world is changing so schools must before we end up as the next Sears or Blockbuster.

It can seem daunting to change a system, and, no, you cannot change that system tomorrow. But, educators can make some shifts in what they do and how they grade tomorrow that can help to move the needle, to improve their Districts, Schools, and classrooms, to put the students they educate at a competitive advantage in our new paradigm.

Stop Giving Zeros

Giving students a zero is one of the most egregious practices that occur in our schools today. No matter how many logical arguments are presented, some see banning zeros as giving students something for nothing. You can point out that grade ranges are 10 points in all instances except from with an F, which is valued at 64 points.

You can remind someone that once a student gets a zero it becomes next to impossible to overcome. Logical argument after logical argument can be made, but the bottom line is some will just not see it logically. Administrators who ban zeros in their Districts may lose some proverbial points with some teachers, but the best can live with it because it is the right thing to do and in the best interest of students.

Test Prep

The quickest way to raise test scores is to have kids practice those test questions again and again. Teach them the tricks of test taking, how to get the easy points and how to avoid the pitfalls that can negatively affect the score they receive. I am embarrassed to say at one point in my career, in an effort to make test prep fun, I made a competition out of it, celebrating the students and teams who mastered components of standardized tests the best. I held pep rallies, I worked hard to ensure that students who did poorly on state tests attended after-school sessions in which they practiced test questions from their Coach test prep books.

My efforts resulted in a short term bump in results. The increase came at a cost though. The payment was a loss of the love of learning, the loss of creativity, the loss of true knowledge and understanding.

There was a time when I felt standardized tests helped to keep schools, and teachers accountable. Now I realize they have done more to damage learning in our country than can be quantified. I understand test prep is a necessary evil in moderation, especially when a student needs to pass a Regents exam or other High School state test required for graduation. That being said, avoid test prep as much as possible, let your students learn, discover, develop and create. This will result in not only a more motivated student, but, in most cases, an organization that will perform better, long term, on whatever silly measure lawmakers decide this week or next is the best way to ensure they are holding us accountable.

Redos

The goal of education is to provide students with the knowledge and skill. If they do not understand a key concept today, but do tomorrow shouldn't they be able to demonstrate that to us? Is it fair to the students who studied the first time, provided a quality product the first time, understood the material the first time?

In my mind yes!!!

If a student is willing to do the assignment better the next time, study again and harder, have it finally make sense after continuing with their studies, have they not demonstrated grit? New assignments and responsibilities do not go away, so continuing to master material that has already been assessed adds to what they need to accomplish.

Allowing redos supports a growth mindset, "I can't do it, yet" If what we are teaching is important in the first place, and kids are willing to keep at it, why should their grade not be reflective of that determination?

Variety of Assessments

Some kids are good test takers, some are not. Offer them a variety of ways to demonstrate their knowledge to you. Knowledge can be assessed based on a one on one conversation with a student. Projects, writings, videos, audio recordings, interviews are all ways that can be considered to determine if a student has actually learned what is required. It may be more work, but ultimately it is a more true and equitable method to assess students. It is certainly better than offering a meaningless extra credit project so students who are poor test takers can use to boost their GPA.

Stop Grading Behavior & Effort

We need to address students who do not behave appropriately in school. We just need to make sure it is not through their grades. A student's English score should be based on their ability to read, write, and communicate. It should not be based on their ability to sit still in class.

Kids who do the work we think they should be doing to meet the goals and objectives of our classes should not have a lower grade. What do they need to learn and how do they demonstrate that knowledge? It is just not fair if the path they took does not match up to what we consider to be the appropriate path. The NBA does not penalize Lebron James if his offseason workout schedule is one not deemed rigorous enough. The bottom line is can he perform on the court.

Feedback Before Grades

Let's be honest with ourselves; grades have very little to do with learning. In fact, they are probably detrimental to the whole learning process. In fact, some educators are experimenting with and supporting gradeless classrooms. This may not be practical in your District or State yet, but the best educators understand that learning is not about grades, it is not about tests scores; learning is about feedback and growth. Learning is a process.

The best educators will not get bogged down with grades and the grading process. The best educators understand the feedback they give students is so much more valuable than the grades. Unfortunately, students and parents often care more about the grade than the feedback because the grade is what will get them on the honor roll, get them the GPA they want, get them into college. Too often teachers provide thoughtful feedback that is not even looked at because students go right to the number.

That is why the number should never be provided until the feedback has been reviewed, and applied. This practice supports a more authentic learning experience.

School leaders need to support and encourage teachers who are willing to make learning the priority, not the number. Educators who consider a different approach, an approach that involves students, one that is flexible, that is rooted in growth rather than conformity with being the educators who will be on the right side of history. They will be the ones who will help to prepare future leaders, thinkers, and creators.

The Teacher

"A number does not determine your worth.
You are far more than a number."

That is a statement that I have been saying more frequently as the years go by. As I share a classroom with more students, each year I see them get more and more focused on the number. If the number isn't close to triple digits, they see themselves as a failure. They believe that they won't get into the right colleges. Teachers will say that they are disappointed. Parents will worry about a "low grade" impacting their child's future. And, ultimately, the student is reduced to tears or decides that they must work harder, sleep less, and do whatever it takes to achieve that perfect score.

That may sound dramatic. But, I just recently lived this. I had given a project to my freshmen that they had a hand in making. We came up with eight different ways they could demonstrate that they read a book (that they chose). So, we wrote the assessment together, I came up with a mini-rubric for assessment, and they began working in class. They had a ton of time on it and it finally came time for them to hand them in.

One group chose to make a soundtrack to the book and explain why the songs related to the themes developed. Their write up was amazing. Their selections were spot on. They had everything, but a minor detail: they forgot to link the songs. So, I filled out the rubric, wrote all of my praise, and underlined the missing part. As I am starting to do more regularly, I am handing back rubrics with feedback, but without the grade. Then, I will put the grade into our portal. At the end of class, I entered the grade, a 98.

The two young ladies' heads slumped as the ding on their phone went off with an alert of the new grade. Fighting off tears--although, not hysterical--they asked what they did wrong. I immediately told them all of the great things and that the number doesn't define them. And, they got a 98! But, they are chasing Principal List, worried about not getting into college. They are freshmen. They are great kids who have been told that the number is important to the game.

I told them they could have the redo, just like our writing. They smiled. I actually changed the grade to the 100, trusting they would get me the link. The did. But, they did it for the number.

Just three years removed from an elementary school where there were no percentage grades, it is now what drives them.

Some may see this as a good thing. We are building kids to have a strong work ethic and a desire to work for success. But, that is a misguided and misunderstood conclusion. We are not driving kids to success. We are driving kids into this perpetual number chase. We are driving them to give up passions, forgo experiences in order to get a number. We are driving kids to take alternative measures in order to keep up with the workload, get all the grade columns filled up.

Notice that not one sentence thus far had the word "learning" in it.

That may sound dramatic or even like a form of sensationalism. But, it is nonetheless the truth.

Grades, how we grade, and the importance we put on grades are the top reasons why students get turned off to learning. They are one of the top reasons why the focus goes to compliance rather than truly learning. And, more importantly, they are one of the top reasons why more and more students are anxious about school.

We can and must do better. We must do better for student health and well being. And, we must do better so that the true focus can return to authentic, intentional, and passionate learning. It starts with reducing the significance of the role a number has in our class.

It may sound counterintuitive because, as teachers, we have always been taught that kids won't do the work unless there is a grade attached to it. Or, that if we want to convey that some assignment is important, we must show that it counts a lot. If we want students to care, we must make it high stakes. But, all we are really doing is feeding into the number culture.

A number never defines a person.

Students are more than a number.

They are people who should be in front of us for the sole purpose to learn, to fuel their passions, and to acquire skills that will allow them to pursue those passions. We must place the emphasis back on learning, rather than a quest for a number.

The number culture is so pervasive that it can even consume the most amazing of kids. Last year, I had the fortune of teaching an amazing group of sophomores. The class was comprised of high achieving, hard workers. All of them were academically successful. In addition to that, among our group was a young lady who is known on a National level for her running ability. In the same class, we had runners who either won individual or team state championships. Add to that one nationally ranked swimmer, a few state ranked swimmers, some baseball and softball players, a member of a championship debate team, and a whole lot of kids who were passionate about community service. They were, in short, an incredible collection of people.

One day, the class was quiet. That wasn't typical at all. They were usually ready to talk about anything and always up for a debate. I walked into the room and saw that they all looked tired.

"What's up?"

They all looked as if they hadn't slept in days. One young lady--the one with the highest grade in the class and an elite athlete as well--broke the silence.

"We were all up until about 3 in the morning getting this outline done."

This wasn't an assignment from my class. I pressed on, knowing exactly what they were doing.

"Why so late? Did you all wait until the last minute?"

"Well, we had to do the readings for the past three nights, a big online quiz, and this outline. And, we also have other classes."

"Why are you stressing the outline?"

"That's a big test grade and we have to do it like he wants us to."

Of course, I saw a bunch of them sitting there, working furiously. I knew what they were doing; they were copying the outline. You see, the assignment was so dense and so time-consuming that many of them had divided the work and still had to stay up until 3 AM. So, they divided the parts of the outline, essentially outsourcing some of their work in order to focus on a manageable part. Then, they bartered, getting the missing pieces from each other.

So, where is the learning here?

I guess we could say that kids learned how to successfully work collaboratively. They learned how to crowdsource information. They learned that the content didn't matter as much as getting the assignment done in a certain way. They learned to comply by any means necessary. Not only are these the brightest, nicest kids you would ever want to meet, but they are also damn good at the game of school.

The true, intended purpose of learning wasn't there because of two reasons. The assignment was unreasonable given the intended content learning targets.

Secondly, it was given for a large grade rather than as a learning tool. The narrative may tell us that kids only care about the grade. But, that has more to do with us not giving them a chance and us not willing to do something better than a century-old practice that has never yielded good learning results.

One of my favorite things about teaching is the fact that every year something different will happen. If you are doing the job right, there will be a twist, new excitement, and even some new dilemmas. It's why I never understood how teachers could say they were bored doing the same thing, year after year. I mean, you can control that, even if you have taught the same grade level for two decades.

Last year--year 20--I had something new happen. About eight weeks into a ten-week quarter, I realized that I didn't have one single grade in the grade book for that same group of kids who were working until 3:00 AM on outlines.

Now, as you can surmise, I have never really been one of those teachers who filled a gradebook with numbers. Obviously, I didn't see the value of homework. Even when I was forced to give it, I would give it minimal value and even "forget" to put it in the book. And, I wasn't about grading every little task or part of the writing process because I figured kids were learning and making mistakes as they progressed towards mastering a skill. Why put a number on learning when we know that it isn't going to be nearly as good as the final product? So, while colleagues may have had close to 20 grades for a given quarter, I would, at most, have six to eight. But, those would be what I thought was meaningful such as final grades on written work after working--and redoing--the process, final projects, presentations, and maybe an occasional traditional test.

But, I never had a blank gradebook.

And, the funny thing was that this was my AP class so it wasn't a question about whether or not they were working. In fact, I would argue that they did more work in those eight weeks than any other group of students in the building. In that time frame, the students worked on a 10-minute group research presentation that not only explores a problem from multiple perspectives, but has to conclude with a solution to fix it. While working towards that presentation, each member had to write their own 1,200-word research paper through a particular lens/perspective on the topic. Once they were done with that, they had to do an individual presentation that solves a problem and write a 2,000 research paper to accompany the presentation.

And, these kids worked. They would use class time to work as many would conference with me. They would email me at all hours of the night, asking for feedback. Sure, all of this would be turned in to College Board as part of their test score, so there was that incentive. But, there was never even a question about what I was going to put on the report card. And, isn't that supposedly what is most important to colleges?

So, what did I do?

I did need to put down a grade on their report card. I had a whole bunch of evidence while conferencing with them during their writing process. I kept a notebook with notes about their progress and what skills they were both conquering and in need of help. I recorded their presentations, took notes on their public speaking skills. Whether I knew it or not, I was entering the world of standards-based grading.

After all of those writing conferences and checking in on their group projects, I had data and a real sense of what they were doing. I was able to go to the standards and check off mastery or still developing on each one. I then calculated that into a number, which went on their report card.

The funny part is that I had not one parent phone call, one inquiry about what their high achieving child was getting, and not one tear from my class. One grade went in the book and there was plenty of evidence to support it at parent-teacher conferences.

We can de-emphasize the number. We must do so.

The Importance of Grade Reform

With the current state of grading, students aren't looking at learning as the objective. Instead, it is about accomplishing tasks. That's a nice way of saying compliance. The industry will complain about students setting up group chats, taking pictures and airdropping answers to each other, or looking to use/ exchange old writing assignments. But, the culture is made that way by the people in charge. By grading every single thing kids do, there is an aura of fear. When a student is fearful, they will not take a chance on learning something. They will do whatever it takes to maintain the grade or pass the course.

The current use of grades is the root cause of cheating in schools. According to a 2017 Rutgers University study that surveyed over 24,000 high school students, 95 percent of respondents admitted to cheating, whether on a test, copying homework, or plagiarizing[5].

That obviously is indicative of the culture we have created. Current grading is forcing kids to make these choices.

With those choices and the pursuit of honor rolls, principal lists, and perceived college requirements, we have all lost sight of the main objective of school. Students cannot do a deep dive into a subject because they have to complete a little assignment for a grade. They can't take a longer time to understand a concept without fear of a bad grade. So, instead of truly working at a skill, they will find the answers rather than learn the answers. Instead of taking time to read a book, a student will search for answers online or on an app to complete the graded ditto, rather than learning the nuances of language that only comes from time to read.

It also forces teachers to make bad choices.

"I need this for a grade in the book."

Too often, assignments are created just for the sake of filling a grade column. That takes away time for the true teaching of skills. That time could be spent continuing to teach, continuing to help a kid refine and master a skill. The focus must shift back to learning.

Finally, reform is needed because the majority of kids are feeling stress. There are still some that scoff at that notion, but with teen suicide climbing at alarming rates and more agencies like the American Psychological Association

5 MacCabe, Donald Lee, et al. Cheating in College: Why Students Do It and What Educators Can Do about It. The Johns Hopkins University Press, 2017.

reporting that 80 percent of students say school causes them high stress, we must act[6]. Driving kids to learn and to push themselves to learn is healthy. Driving kids to hit a number is not.

Ways to Reform Grades in Your Classroom

Even if you don't want to dive right into the deep end with Standards Based Gradings, there are many ways to develop a culture of learning and reframing the role of grades in a class.

Explicitly Remove the Fear

Perhaps one of the most overlooked techniques in teaching is being explicit with intentions. Perhaps it is a fear within teachers that stems from not wanting to fail. If one puts themselves out there with clarity and purpose and it doesn't work, then what?

I get that. But, having failed epically many times, I can say, with certainty, that students respect you more, will do more, and be more willing to do harder stuff if you are explicit with your intentions. So, on the first day of school, I will tell every class that I will never hold their grade over their head. Ever. I give my mantra about them being more than a number and that I want them to take chances and to learn. I tell them about my redo policies, the fact that I will not grade everything they do, and that I expect them to fail at things on their first try. I want them to take chances with their writing and not hand in the cookie cutter pieces that the industry has taught them during their academic careers.

I say the same thing on parent night. And, I keep saying it during the first weeks of school as students are naturally skeptical about this. Since they entered the secondary level, they have been held hostage with their grades. They have been told that those numbers matter. And now here I am telling them that this class won't be that way.

So, then, I have to prove my words with my practices.

---

6 "American Psychological Association Survey Shows Teen Stress Rivals That of Adults." American Psychological Association, American Psychological Association, www.apa.org/news/press/releases/2014/02/teen-stress.aspx.

Don't Grade Everything

The first practice comes up during the first week when I have them write something for me in class. We generate a quick menu of options for them to write about, but they could really write me anything. Every year, it is the same conversation, like a scene from Bill Murray's classic, Groundhogs Day.

"Are you grading this?"

"Good question, but no. This is for me to see what kind of writer you are and what kind of stuff we can do this year."

"It's really not going to count?"

"No, like I said, your work and, more importantly, you are not a number. This is about the craft of writing, how we communicate, and how we can grow. Those skills are the ones that not only help you do anything in your life, but can, literally, change the world. No grade. You are practicing, showing me. How can I place a value on something I haven't taught or we haven't worked on together? This is your start."

Ok, so maybe that's the Cliff Notes version of the conversation, but that is the general idea.

After a while, it becomes second nature to kids. We are practicing and developing skills. That is the purpose of our class. That is what matters. Grading everything will only limit the practice. It's like coaching a baseball team. We have more practices than games. In those practices, I have players working on different skills and techniques like hitting the ball to the opposite field or taking different routes to field a ball. Practice allows for that. They aren't trying new things in a game, when the score comes into play, that they are not comfortable with. We adults are the same way. If someone wanted to learn how to code and design their own website, they wouldn't go buy a domain, code a website, and have it as an integral part of their business, where the score is kept by dollars and cents. Instead, a person would take a course, experiment with code and create dummy sites. They would practice different techniques to really learn the skill without the pressure of the score. People learn better that way. Why do we think kids are any different?

Value Process/Feedback

Every education guru will talk about process. Some will use different words such as differentiate, multiple intelligences, or even as simple as options, but all of that comes down to valuing the process of learning and giving students feedback along the way.

It may sound simplistic and we have heard it a bajillion times, but it is worth repeating.

All students learn differently and at different paces.

As teachers, we must provide an environment that allows for this to happen. For far too long, the secondary education field has been dominated by the top-down approach. Teacher lectures or presents, students produce, teacher grades, rinse and repeat. That is a one-size, hardly fits anybody type of approach.

Instead, we must set up our classrooms to value the process of learning, the process of experiencing failure, and the process in which we respond to failure. We must continue that process to ingrain that "stick-to-it-iveness" that we want our kids to have and further it so that when they finish something, they know it is not the end. They can revise and improve.

As a teacher of English, this is easy. Writing isn't assigned. It is taught. It is practiced. Many teachers like to say they go over the writing process with kids. You know the famous: brainstorm, draft, revise, edit, publish. They aren't lying. They go over it and then assign kids an essay to write.

That is not the writing process. We must teach writing, just like other content area teachers have to teach skills. My classroom, today, looks like orchestrated chaos; at least I hope it has the aura of orchestrated. Kids are working on a writing piece. They, in the end, chose their topic based on our topic generation activities. They are working through writing the draft. Each day--or almost each day--they are conferencing with me, getting feedback, asking me questions about how to improve, and seeing if their attempts at different writing techniques we have learned in class actually worked for them in this setting.

When they are done, they go into revision mode. We conference about how they can make their points more clearly. Could they restructure their argument? Could they use different wording? Could they break up the paragraphs more so their points are more effectively read?

Those questions and those skills being developed are important. They are a part of a process. Students are being given the opportunity to go through that process without the fear of being graded. Sure, they have a rubric to guide them so they can see where they stand, but our focus is on taking their writing and making it more impactful. So, there is more effort in their writing because they know they can take chances and try things. There is no one telling them what to do, how to do it, and grading them on each little part. The result is more authentic pieces. The result is more confident and skilled writers because they were allowed to practice.

Every content area can do this. It doesn't matter the course--a teacher can structure their classes to allow learning without grading, and often penalizing, a kid during the process of acquiring a skill.

Options and Voice
If we want to show students that we are serious about the process of learning rather than the grading of learning, we must allow them multiple pathways to demonstrate their mastery. Whether it is an English Teacher allowing students to pick their own argument topic to research, explore, and write about, or a science teacher allowing students to conduct different experiments within a given unit, students will value the learning more and want to show what they have learned. More importantly, they will understand that learning is a process that is rarely linear. We must give students options. We must allow them to have a voice in what we do.

That is difficult for the people who like to have their copies made in the summer, but it is the only way to truly, authentically assess kids. After a reading unit--or a unit in a content area--there is absolutely no harm in asking kids for their ideas about demonstrating their comprehension. You could share your ideas with them and invite them to either add to them or modify them. In the end, students will buy into an assessment that they know is about demonstrating and furthering their learning rather than trying to "get them" for what they failed to do.

I've said it quite a bit over the past few years, but I need to say it here. If we aren't allowing redos in school, then what is our purpose?

My absolute favorite part of "Meet the Teacher Night" is when I see surprised nods of parents towards each other before looking back at me. This always happens after I tell them that their children can rewrite anything, as many times as they want, until they get a 100. There is no set limit. There is no time frame, other than when we have to post final grades at the end of each quarter. I go on to tell them that writing is a process and the only way to learn and to improve as a writer is to keep doing it, keep trying to improve on newly taught skills, and keep learning from mistakes. That is the only way to achieve mastery.

The same goes for most tests, quizzes, and projects. Students have all quarter to redo most work to demonstrate mastery. And, yes, they can get a 100 if they do so.

Inevitably, there are some reading these words right now who are giving "the eye rolls", thinking that I am "one of those". I am soft and just want students to like me. They probably think that I am a pushover and don't have high expectations.

But, giving students the opportunity to redo an assignment isn't weak. It is telling the student that the skills needed to complete the assignment are important. They are so important–so valued–that the students should put in the time to learn them. They will need them. The skills are not something that they can temporarily use and then forget for the rest of their lives.

These skills matter much more than a number in a grade book. They matter so much that we won't be offering a redo for just a portion of credit; we will offer it until they receive a 100. That takes away the carrot of the grade and places the focus on the skills to be learned.

They matter so much that if students are willing to put in the work to redo the assignment–relearn it or learn the skills better–than I am willing to put in the work to discuss, reteach, and reassess. Putting a number in a grade book would be so much easier, but this would be a signal that numbers and finality are more important than learning.

The counterargument to redos is the idea that we don't get a redo in real life; we don't get second chances with deadlines, responsibilities, and with jobs. There are two ways to look at it. First, school is about preparing students. If a student hasn't learned the material and hasn't learned how to apply that material, how, exactly, is he/she prepared for the real world?

Perhaps the intention of preparing a student for the real world is genuine; you mean well. But, the message sent is really this: a kid should get it right the first time; it was communicated to them by a bad grade. The intention of developing a sense of responsibility shouldn't supersede the simple fact that you, as the Teacher, have no real proof whether or not that kid mastered the skills you were teaching because you chose to move on. They are moving on without a skill.

The second reason is actually the more logical reason. We do get redo's in almost everything in life.

Yes, there are jobs that come with a "life and death" mentality and consequence. But, those jobs aren't given out until there are thousands of hours of simulation time. In other words, the people doing the most dangerous jobs must put in thousands of hours in order to master a skill. It is only until they demonstrate mastery that they can go into the field and do it for real.

And, that's the extreme jobs. Those less stressful jobs have the same thing. People aren't elevated into the high-end positions where decisions can make or break companies until they learn the craft and, as the cliché goes, climb the corporate ladder. Craftsmen serve apprenticeships in order to master their skills. Athletes put in hours upon hours of practice time to master their craft. There is a time in every walk of professional life built in for failure. That failure allows for the opportunity to learn and grow.

In every walk of life, there is a culture of learning and a culture of redo until the skill is mastered.

Education–the institution that is supposed to prepare kids for this world–must fully adopt this culture.

Sadly, education, as a whole, has not.

That doesn't mean to ignore the genre of "one and done" exercises that would prepare kids for on-demand testing. They just shouldn't be the norm. We must put the purpose of school into perspective. School isn't about achieving grades; it is about achieving learning.

That is why all of this grade reform matters. We want to put the focus back onto learning so kids don't feel the need to group chat for answers, sit in the cafeteria and copy homework, or look for summaries online. Instead, they will do things because they matter and that they care about it. And, we can show that equally because we aren't just giving "gotcha" assignments. We are allowing them to have a voice in them. We are giving feedback along the way. And, we are allowing for redo's until they show mastery. If we do all of that, we will show our kids the true purpose of school.

Grading Reform Takeaways for Admins

→ Learning is a process, not a moment in time.

→ Expectations should always be clear. Let students know exactly what they need to learn and how they will demonstrate that knowledge.

→ Allow redos.

→ Zeros are mathematically illogical.

→ Never use grades as a consequence for poor behavior.

→ When it becomes about the number, it is at the cost of true learning.

→ Always provide feedback before you give the grade.

→ Offer different ways for students to demonstrate understanding of the goals and objectives of your class.

→ Never penalize grades because of performance or lack of homework (I know, I know that was the last chapter but it is that important to remember!)

→ Our priority as educators is to teach and inspire students not rank them.

Grading Reform Takeaways for Teachers

→ Students are more than a number. Set that environment so they believe it.

→ Numbers do not motivate learning; they motivate compliance.

→ An emphasis on numbers not only promotes compliance, it heightens student anxiety.

→ If we want learning to be authentic, we must build in opportunities that allow kids to learn from failure without fear of a number being attached to that natural part of the learning process.

→ Feedback should always be given and reviewed before a grade is given.

→ Giving students a voice in how they are assessed will give a more realistic view of what they have mastered.

→ A redo isn't a sign of weakness; it shows that you value the skill being taught so much that you want the student to keep working so it is mastered.

→ The real world allows time for practice, redos, and mastery, especially the highest pressured professions.

VOICES FROM THE FIELD...

Laura Robb, Educator

Do Grades Measure Learning?

Ask that question during a faculty meeting and tension increases as teachers explain their positions. Perhaps frustration develops because grading criteria varies among teachers or some use grades as punishments. Perhaps, anxiety rises whenever educators state that test grades measure students' success or failure to learn. However, like me, there are educators who wonder whether grades are the primary indicator of learning.

Unfortunately, in many schools across our country, teachers give zeros to students who don't complete work and take points off late homework and writing assignments. For a semester grade, some teachers average a student's low grades at the start of a semester with a string of A's earned during the last several weeks. The hope is zeroes and low grades will motivate students to develop responsibility and work hard while preparing them for the "real world." This. Doesn't. Work.

Today, many teachers, administrators, and parents have begun to question whether grades are fair, reliable from school to school, show what students know, and motivate students to learn. You can reflect on grading and students' learning by discussing two questions with colleagues: What is the purpose of school? How does instruction prepare students for their future studies and career choices?

For me, the purpose of school is to develop experiences that invite students to collaborate and communicate, analyze information, and tap into their creativity. These are skills students will need to solve tough problems like: water and food shortages, pandemics, and overpopulation. Ideally, learning experiences should provide students with opportunities to practice and refine these skills while reading, researching, writing, discussing, sharing, and using technology.

So, how does a traditional grading system fit into this purpose? I have trouble with grades as punishments and grades not reflecting progress. However, I have no trouble with grades as long as they become one type of assessment among many formative assessments: kid watching notes, teacher-student conferences, self-evaluations, authentic reading and writing, project-based learning, integrating technology, and setting goals and designing a plan for reaching them.

If we want to prepare students for their futures, then it's time to rethink grading practices that instill discouragement instead of hope, a desire to learn, and develop students' ability to become creative problem solvers.

7

Encouraging Innovation &

Taking Instructional Risks

"Mediocrity is always invisible until passion shows up and exposes it." ~ Graham Cooke

A few years ago, Dave Rendall, author of The Freak Factor, spoke to our district during our professional development day. During his inspiring talk, he said to the crowd of 600-plus teachers, "the further you deviate from the norm, the more pressure there will be from others to conform."

Rendall's words were impactful and quite true. Anyone in education who dares to try something new is often met with resistance from those who want you to do things the way they were always done. That pressure can squelch innovation and stop teachers from the necessary taking instructional risks that could not only more effectively teach students, but leave them with an impactful experience they will remember forever.

In order to better prepare our students, in order to make their classroom experience more relevant and engaging, educators must be more willing than ever before to be innovative. We must challenge past practices, truly decide whether they are still valuable to kids, no matter how long they have been in practice.

Administrators must work to remove that fear of taking a chance, of doing something new, of what will happen if something innovative fails. The Admin must create an environment where test scores don't guide decision making and the curriculum is not stifling to our teachers creativity. They must be willing to allow teachers to use that professional development to do new things, to challenge the convention, the move beyond mediocrity, and give kids an experience they will never forget.

Teachers must take the accepting environment created by the administrator and take those risks. They must continually look to find new ideas, new ways to engage kids, new, more creative ways to deliver instruction. The teacher cannot be afraid to put themselves out there, explain why they are doing things differently, be honest with kids when taking a risk, and to be willing to fail.

The Admin

Growth as a leader, as an educator, is essential if we are going to make schools all they can be and all that our kids deserve. The biggest step towards that growth is often, simple--letting go. Letting go of control in the classroom, letting go of control in the building you run, letting go in the District you are charged with leading.

Teachers are told by their principals that they need to "be more student-centered" or encourage students to "own" their learning. Certainly, great advice, but when it comes from a dictatorial principal or District leader who is afraid to give their teacher autonomy in what they do in their classrooms, it comes off as disingenuous.

How can a teacher be "the guide on the side" when their sage of a principal is orchestrating their every move, measuring them by scores on a standardized test, or criticizing them for deviating from the play or plan book?

Letting go is hard to do. It is much easier to follow the script, to take out your hammer when things do not go according to plan. We can justify it in our minds. Sometimes it manifests as the teacher who checks off the curricular boxes, despite knowing a different approach is probably what his students need. Sometimes it is the principal who collects lesson plans demanding they include goals and objectives that are perfectly aligned to the cumbersome state standards.

It is strange that in our field so many of us are so worried about complying, following the rules, checking all the boxes of what is supposed to be done.

Why is it that so many well-meaning educators are afraid to deviate from the script?

Administrators need to motivate, empower, guide, and help bring the best out in their teachers, not threaten, demand, or declare.

The best teachers plan, read, learn, observe, attend workshops, go the extra mile, not because if they become better, they will make more and not because if they don't improve, they will be fired. They choose to cherish the profession because, for them, it is a duty, a responsibility, and, for the very best, a glorious opportunity to make a difference in a life every single year, every single day.

Imagine waking up each morning with the opportunity to be a hero for someone, to change the trajectory of a life, to achieve immortality in the memories of those you work with.

If you are reading this, chances are you are an educator and you are one of the lucky few who have that opportunity, every single day!

What a shame to squander that, as so many do by counting down the days until the next break or, worse, the final break. What a shame to mindlessly provide the same lessons year after year, drinking from the same coffee mug, in the same room, complaining about how much worse kids are each year while holding court in a dated faculty room sitting on furniture that is one step away from the local dump.

THE **TEACHER** & THE **ADMIN**

I may be an optimist, but I would like to think that most teachers, administrators, even the most jaded, even the most negative, and even the most apathetic got into the profession, not because of the summers and snow days, and certainly not for the pay, but rather to do some good. To have a purpose in life, to make a difference.

Many teachers year after year have been told how to do things by: an education department that is not grounded in reality; principals just trying to keep their heads above water; parents who are not worried about learning and inspiration, but rather grades, awards, and opportunities for their children; central office staff who have forgotten what is like to be in the classroom.

This can wear you down, and unless someone wakes you up, or you wake yourself up, you quickly learn how to play the game, how to fit in, how to conform. How can administrators expect teachers to be about innovation and creativity when they themselves are about conformity and control?

Schools need to change!

Our world is changing and if we do not change with it, schools as we know it will be replaced.

The achievement gap is not shrinking, poor students are less likely to find success than their more affluent counterparts.

Students of color are more likely to be jailed, less likely to attend college.

Kids become less and less engaged as they progress through schools.

I am afraid that kids are successful not because of school, but despite it.

The scary thing about growth as a professional is you start to realize how much you don't know, the solutions are not black and white, the answers are complex, and success is a moving target.
You have two choices when you come to grips with this realization. You can complain, you can become that curmudgeon, you can become bitter, or you

can take off your damn gloves, get your hands dirty, and be a warrior that does all you can to make things better for kids.

You can be the administrator that says I know these standardized tests are damaging, they do not measure what they should be measuring. You can stick to your beliefs and fight a system that measures your students, your teachers, your school, and you as if you were all robots filling in dots.

What type of educator do you want to be?

One who plays by the rules of a broken game, who gets by, collects a nice pension, retires at 55 after a few obligatory awards?

Or one who does something that will be remembered, a pioneer, a thinker, one who takes chances on students, on teachers, on yourself?

You can be a badass; it is not easy, it is not comfortable, people and systems will try to knock you down.

I don't know about you, but I would rather live a career that matters, rather than work a job that pays the bills.

Administrators, it is time to start trusting your teachers. Build them up and challenge them to be divergent in their thinking. Give your teacher's permission to experiment, to take risks, to try something that is out of your comfort zone.

Once you have given that permission, I see it as the administrator's job, to help your teachers figure out a way to get it done.

It is the administrator's job to promote teachers' successes and shield them from their failures.

Administrators cannot expect teachers to take chances on kids if they do not take chances on their teachers. Administrators cannot ask teachers to look for strengths in students, forgive their indiscretions, to take things less personally if they do not reciprocate that approach with the staff in their buildings.

It is easier said than done; trust me I struggle with this every day. I am quick to write off a teacher who dared to go against me, show a lack of respect, have a bad day, month, or year.

I once forced a young teacher out of the door of the small school I was principal of because he had the nerve to question what I thought was a great idea behind my back.

It was a faculty meeting in my first year as a principal. I was trying to be creative and help my team overcome the February blues, time that most Northeastern educators face as the long hard winter seems to have no end in sight and everyone is on your nerves. I decided I would propose a job swap. Everyone, including me, would switch their role in the school for a day. I was even considering including the custodians and secretaries in this experiment. That's when a young teacher let it be known how he felt about me and the idea. Of course, in schools, nothing stays secret long and his snide remarks got back to me shortly. Did I ask him about his remarks? Did I ask him for other ideas? Did I try to see the positive in him? Try to coach him? No, No, and NOOOOO.

I modeled what an insecure and inexperienced principal would do. I waited for the opportunity to get even. When he handled a difficult parent situation poorly I didn't coach him, I wrote him up. When he had trouble with classroom management I didn't offer support, I offered judgment and poor evaluations. And, when his test scores came back poorly I brought it to our test conscious superintendent and asked that he be let go.

Was he right for the profession? I guess I will never know because I took his immature remark personally, I did exactly what I insist teachers never do to kids. I quit on him. I made my mind up about who he was and that was not someone I wanted on my team.

Have I acted with vengeance rather than kindness since this incident? Unfortunately, yes, but I am working each day to get better, to look for the good in those I lead and pull it out of them.

How can an administrator foster that trust, that willingness to take risks to ensure that your school is one that is innovative?

As a district leader, I have tried to listen, to support, and encourage creativity. It starts with being open, with a willingness to accept that others may have a better idea and a plan than you do.

I see the single most important step that an administrator can take is to break down the walls that separate our teachers from each other and from all of the other amazing educators in our field. That is when innovation grows exponentially.

Last year our District established the North Rockland "Twitter Challenge". It was completely voluntary so I was worried that no one would participate.

I was able to generate some buzz with teaser emails and posters. Here is an example of one of our teaser emails:

Many of our colleagues in North Rockland have started to explore Twitter as a means to connect with other educators, find/share ideas, and obtain a plethora of educational resources. I was skeptical at first, but have been shocked by how much I have learned from other educators on Twitter in the past couple of months! I have attached an article that describes some of the Twitter basics.

Stay tuned for the North Rockland Twitter Challenge coming soon! Those who complete the challenge will receive a special surprise!!!!

I hope everyone had a nice long weekend and are ready for another great week as an educator in North Rockland!

Each day, a different Twitter task was sent to the staff to help them become familiar with the tool and see the value in using it as a means to improve their instructional practices and connecting with other educators. Upon completion of the challenge, teachers received a digital badge and a NR Twitter pin. I also randomly selected 20 teachers (over 100 completed the challenge) who were awarded an extra prep period.

THE **TEACHER** & THE **ADMIN**

I was the "Sub" teacher and initially saw covering classes as a way to give back to teachers and to reconnect with kids. Little did I know at the time that it would serve as the best professional development that I would receive the entire year. The opportunity to live what teachers live, to speak to kids, to test theory in practice gave me insights that could never have been achieved from my office or even in traditional visits to the schools.

The Twitter Challenge provided my teachers with the opportunity to connect with educators in our District as well as outside the District. By interacting with other educators, connections were built, a sense of camaraderie, a renewed pride in the profession.

Twitter exposed our teachers to new ideas, methods, approaches.

I doubt this resource would have taken root like it did had they been a directive that was mandated by "central." The organic sharing and growth have proved to be authentic. It has continued to build and teachers seemed hungry for more.

This led to our second challenge in as many years, the Pineapple challenge. This is based on an article and idea of Pineapple Charts developed by Jennifer Gonzalez.

Pineapple charts are a concept in which teachers visit other classrooms to learn from and get ideas from one another without the pressure of a supervisor being part of the process. It is basically teachers watching other teachers in action.

The structure was similar, complete the tasks in the challenge and receive a NR Pineapple pin, a digital badge and hours of in-service credit.

North Rockland Pineapple Challenge

Example Promo Emails

The Pineapple Challenge will be starting after the break! The format and checklist will be provided shortly. If you would like to get a jump start you can create a Pineapple sign for your door.

Bonus points for creativity but if you are as unartistic as I am you can simply print a picture of a Pineapple and hang it on your door.

I truly believe that you have much more to learn from each other than from any PD we could possibly offer. I am happy that so many of you are considering joining the challenge!

Check out this video that discusses the value of learning from other teachers.

Requirements to complete the challenge:
- *Read this article on the origins of pineapple charts*
- *Watch this video on the value of peer observations*
- *Watch this inspirational TED Talk by Rita Pierson*
- *Create a pineapple sign for your door that indicates you are participating in the challenge, you can be as elaborate or as simple as you like. If you think you have the most creative, inspirational, or crafty pineapple snap a pic and email it to kelicello@northrockland.org or Tweet it to #nrcsdchat or #NRpineapple . The top pineapple will win a special surprise.*
- *Observe three or more teachers in action*
- *Have three or more teachers observe you*

Directions:
- *Hang the pineapple on your door.*
- *Accept the pineapple calendar email invite so you can add to the calendar.*
- *Indicate on the "Pineapple calendar" for your building when you are willing to have visitors to your class. You can find the building calendars and directions here. You can also visit the calendar to determine who will be visiting.*
- *Fill out the form found here indicating you have completed the challenge. There is no paperwork to hand in this challenge, it is based on professionalism. When you finish, let me know I trust you.*

> *Those who complete the challenge will be awarded:*
> - *3 CTLE hours*
> - *3 In-service hours*
> - *NR Pineapple Challenge pin*
> - *Digital badge for your email or website*
>
> *Other information:*
> - *The goal is to learn and get ideas from other teachers, it is not to critique others or tell them how to do it better.*
> - *This challenge is for teachers, not administrators.*
> - *If you are always open to others observing you write "Always" on your door pineapple sign.*
> - *You do not have to turn anything in, just complete the form so you can be awarded your hours, pin, and digital badge.*
> - *If you have a teacher you would like to see but can not get coverage for your class or your preps do not match up, email me the time you would like to observe and I will coordinate a date that I will cover your class for you.*
> - *Bonus points for those who provide their favorite pineapple based dishes for the faculty room or main office.*

PDF version of Pineapple Challenge may be found on our website
https://theteacherandtheadmin.com

I was able to work with our District Technology Specialist Craig Mantin and my assistant Diane Serano to develop a web site that allowed teachers to indicate times when they would welcome other teachers to watch them teach.

In retrospect, I would probably simplify the process. Although we have had several teachers complete the challenge, next time I would probably ask teachers who wanted to participate to put a pineapple on their door, and hook up with other teachers with pineapples on their doors to coordinate visits. It has been a little cumbersome and confusing for the teachers to use the electronic pineapple chart. That being said, getting my teachers to learn from each other has fostered growth and innovation.

Another way to promote innovation in your District is by investing in professional development. Getting your people out of the District, out of the county, and even out of the State can serve as a means to motivate, to excite, to spark interest and ideas that would never happen without supporting them in an effort to increase the circle of educational minds they hear from, and connect with.

A team visit to the Ron Clark Academy has reinvigorated one of our 4-6 elementary schools. Student photographers have their pictures of their classmates, teachers, and school proudly displayed in the hallways. It is not uncommon to see teachers standing on their desks to deliver a lesson and students ringing bells or banging drums to celebrate classmates. Next year, they will be implementing a Harry Potter-like house system.

Last summer, a group of teachers came back from the "Get Your Teach On" Conference so excited that they have spread the career-changing experience (their words not mine) to others in our District with some of the best professional development sessions I have ever seen. I was excited about the incredible transformation days they facilitated with their students and the #Northrockourschools movement they started. This is a day where teachers who participated in their sessions are asked to go out of their comfort zone for a day.

This day proved to be one where rooms, hallways, and entire schools were transformed into a specific theme. It didn't matter if it was Super Bowl theme, Toy Story, or NASCAR, students were presented with rigorous lessons that connected with the themes. Teachers reported that not only did discipline issues decline and excitement increased, but actual learning and retention was at an all-time high during their transformation day.

I have seen some truly innovative practices going in my District:

- Student-led businesses with 3rd graders serving as CEOs
- STEM creations highlighted at a District STEM fair
- Classroom Transformations
- Learning Academies such as Art Academy, Finance Academy, Stem Academy, to name a few
- District Fitness days
- A student help desk that solves computer issues.

The list goes on and on. The thing is these great experiences are in most cases not led by me or other administrators. They are the brainchild of our teachers, our students, and our support staff.

I believe it is the job of administrators to expose those they lead to other educators, to experts in the field, and other resources that peak interest and help spread ideas. Good administrators support teachers, let them know it is ok to take risks.

The best administrators not only support risk-taking, but also help provide teachers with the resources to make their vision a reality, no matter how wild those ideas may seem.

School can be a boring place if everyone does the same thing everyday.

It's ok for us to be different, to support different, to encourage different. In fact, it is essential if we are going to survive as a profession.

The Teacher

It does take a sort of bravery to break free from the commonality that is education. In an industry over a century old, there are so many traditions, so many "past practices", and so many built-in routines that can anchor even the strongest. And, history should never be ignored. There is always something to be learned from it. We can hold on to good virtues. We can hold on to the idealism that education represents.

The virtue of education being the great equalizer is something that history teaches us. It is something that we, the classroom leaders, must keep in our minds every single second we are in a classroom full of kids. If we are doing our jobs right, we are giving each kid a chance to go out in the world, find their own passion, and make a true impact on the world. History shows us this. That part of the tradition of the education field should be held sacred. It should guide us each and every day.

I see this every day, but the most powerful example of this was when I was teaching my ESL students. This was a group of students, as I've said before, who were working twice as hard as everyone else. They were learning a new language, translating content, translating what they wanted to say, and then expressing it in a new language. And, they were expected to take the same assessments as every other kid. At first, I thought it was unfair. Even as I was challenging them and telling them that it was us against the world, there was something in the back of my head that kept thinking that I wished it was easier for them.

One young lady changed my thinking. She was in my 10th grade class and was driven. She knew exactly what she wanted to do. She wanted to be a nurse. She wrote about how it was something she always dreamed about ever since she was a small kid in the Dominican Republic, or "The D.R." as all of my kids would say. She came to the United States with her family for a better way and landed in a ninth grade sheltered class, where most kids had limited English. She worked hard. Although she wasn't my student at that point, her teacher would always tell me about this young lady who was always writing, always working, and pushing herself. She was always asking for feedback and always said that she wanted out of ESL. I wasn't surprised when she landed in my class for 10th grade.

Early in the year, the class hit the frustration point that I had grown accustomed to. We were reading a poem and kids were frustrated. They were shutting down. I went into my "Us against the World" speech and told them the truth; they were working twice as hard.

This young lady raised her hand.

"Mr. Armida, I want to say something if that's ok."

She was one of the few who called me by "Mr. Armida", as most would just say "mister".

"Absolutely, go for it."

"I know you are saying that we are working hard, but we have no choice. If any of us wants to do anything in this country, we have to work. We have to learn the language. We have to be better. We can't complain if we want to be seen as equal."

It was the most beautiful thing a student has ever said in my classroom.

Most of the kids in the class went back to the poem and tried hard, asking questions. After class, I called her up to my desk.

"That was awesome. I am proud that you said that to everyone. You made a difference."

"It's true. I came here to get an education because that will give me the opportunity to be a nurse and help people."

"You're going to be a great nurse."

That young lady finished her 10th grade year with me and was then fully out of the ESL program, taking her 11th grade class in the mainstream, achieving a master score on the English Regents. She took our college course for her senior year and went off to college.

Any time I feel like our industry needs to be completely changed, I think of her. There is one tradition worth holding onto and it is the idealism that education is the great equalizer. That tradition drives me and many others to make the industry better; we must be better for kids. We must give them every opportunity to learn meaningful content in order to take on the world.

And, that is only the tradition that I will honor in education.

The rest depends upon whether or not the practice is best for kids.

Thankfully, the paradigm seems to be shifting in the field. More and more Administrators are encouraging their teachers to break from the traditions of drill and skill, rote exercises, and standard, top-down classroom instruction. More teachers are getting on board as well. But, there is still a significant pull to stay the same. Walk into any teacher's lounge and that pull feels like quicksand. Start working on something innovative or have kids actually be excited about something and the comments will come flying at you from every relic that works in your building. It happened to me when I first started out. It continues to happen 21 years later.

As an English Teacher, there is a delicate battle that takes place about what literature is worthy enough to read. I once toed the line of curriculum, which was filled with so many pieces of literature that I had zero interest in reading, let alone teaching. The Odyssey? Ugh. Romeo and Juliet? Even worse. Ok, nothing is worse than The Odyssey, but you get the idea.

Even worse, the curriculum stated that we would have to make kids fill out reading logs, make sticky notes, and do packets of questions, all in an effort to prove that they were reading these boring books that had little relevance in their lives. Sure, some kids would actually like them and I, as a teacher, could make anything interesting enough to follow along, but all of that time and my energy was spent getting kids through something rather than doing something that could be really meaningful. If we are focused on skills, why would we get so caught up on the traditional reading pieces?

Years ago, before I became Department Coordinator, I was asked to be on our curriculum writing committee. It was a group of us charged with rewriting the curriculum to meet the changing New York State Standards. I saw it as an opportunity to fight for kids and make things more interesting. Some of my older colleagues saw it differently. When the subject of what books to teach came up, I brought up the idea of growing the booklist and allowing for more choice. I brought up the idea of focusing on writing and using texts as mentor pieces to help develop their writing skills. One colleague was violently opposed to this. I may be putting that mildly.

"Kids need to read the classics. I read them. My parents read them. They have been read for hundreds of years. We are not going to dumb it down just it is easier for them and you."

I remember thinking, "wait? Did she just call me lazy?"

But, I decided to engage.

"What does it matter what kids read as long as we are teaching skills? Maybe if we get them interested in actually reading, they may be more into the classics. But, we are not supposed to be teaching units on a certain book. The standards are skills."

"No, we've done things this way forever and it has worked. We are not going to change."

It was then that I felt validated in what I had been doing over the years. Secretly, I had been doing my own thing because I felt that it was best for kids. Now, I had the easy out because it was the ESL class and I had freedom. But, even when I was given a section outside of ESL, I would find things that I felt would engage kids better. As long as I was focused on skill development, the canvas on which I painted them on is irrelevant.

But, I don't want to downplay the courage it takes in order to be innovative and take instructional risks. You are flying against a 100 years' worth of - "we always did it this way" and against a climate where there is more parental criticism and spotlight put into what is being done in the classroom. It is easier to blend in. It will be less of a headache, less work, and less anxiety. There will be minimal pressure because you can hide behind curriculum and tradition.

I often have to check myself because I have always just sort of did that and figured I would deal with any consequences later. I never thought about job security or anything because I always fell back on the idea that if I was doing what was right for kids, focused on their skill development, and was honest with them and their parents, there wouldn't be a negative. I was right, but I can see why someone is fearful to take such a leap. Words like tenure loom heavy over people. Having to do additional work is burdensome considering the already immense workload. It is often difficult to stand by yourself, even if it is for the right reasons. And, change by its very nature is scary. The peace from hiding behind the status quo and having the ability to punch in and punch out can be alluring.

The trade-off for that seeming peace is simple: you won't be making one bit of difference for kids.

162

You won't push them forward. You won't make them value learning. You won't inspire passions or take advantage of their passions in order to get them to work harder than they ever thought they could or would. You won't be preparing them for tomorrow's world. Instead, you'll be preparing them for the world of decades ago.

So, how do you prepare yourself to take a risk? How do you explain? How do you jump into something scary, but something that will make you a better educator and, more importantly, gives your students a memorable and meaningful experience?

Honesty

One of the best lessons I learned from my department chair during the early years of my career was that I didn't have all of the answers. It was alright to tell kids that I wasn't all knowing and that it was ok to not know everything. He told me that kids would respect me more for the honesty and then benefit from watching me acquire the knowledge. Like everything else, he was right.

That applies to educational risks. While I did hide things the things I did from colleagues, I was always honest with my students. I would—and still do—tell them why we were doing something different. I would give the rationale, the list of skills we would be working on, and why this route would be the best, most engaging one for them. I would then invite them to give me their ideas. We'd modify the plan together.

This happened recently—in year 21—when I finally decided to act on something I have long held true. We teach books at kids. We come in with our prepared points and things we want them to get out of literature, rather than giving them skills to be able to make their own, genuine connections. We lead them to points, thinking that teenagers should have the same connection to words that we have as 40-something-year-olds. But, even at a point in my career where I am comfortable taking risks, doing something so different was definitely nerve-wracking.

I sought out one of my colleagues who is a fellow risk taker. I am fortunate to work with Lauren Madden, a young English Teacher, who is always ready to try something new. She is always looking to make even her most successful lessons better and more relevant. She tries new things, does the research on her new ideas, and then goes into the classroom and excites kids. I explained to her my feelings about how we teach the book. She agreed and started talking about how she was teaching the book, The Very True Diary of a Part-Time Indian by Sherman Alexie. Lauren had asked for our district to order it because she had taught it in her previous district and knew her kids would love it. But, her approach was far from traditional.

Lauren gave her kids options of how to read the book. She would read aloud with the whole class or a group. Groups could read to each other. Kids could read silently. Or, they could listen to the audio. There wouldn't be quizzes or worksheets. They would discuss the book through Socratic Seminars or in small groups. The topics would be whatever the kids found relatable.

As I was hearing her tell me all of this, I said, "that book sounds awesome. I think I want to read it with my 9th graders. I just have to read it first."

Then, I said something I had always wanted to say out loud, "I wish I could just read it with them and experience it like they would."

Lauren immediately said, "you should do that. Why not?"

Why not?

Exactly.

It was an instructional risk because I would be teaching a book that I had no idea where it was going. Essentially, I would come in each day without a plan for content or even skill for that matter. Our reading days would be a shared experience and then I would allow their connections to guide me. I'd also model for them how I figure things out when I read and how I make connections. Not only would the book be more relevant to them, but the lessons would be as well. And, by taking the no worksheet approach, we are developing a culture where reading is valued and students are treated like human beings.

The rationale behind it is excellent. It is what is best for kids. But, I had to be honest with the kids too. So, I went into class the next day and handed out the books.

"This could be one of the best things I do as a teacher or it could fail miserably. I really think it will be on the best. Who's with me?"

All 25 kids raised their hands. Ok, I had them. I kept going.

"Confession. I have never read this book before."

Some kids gave me the look of disbelief.

"Seriously, I have never read it. I am going to read it with you. There's a lot of reasons why I am doing it this way…"

I explained to them all. I told them that I believe in this, but this was a risk. I was willing to take it because I truly believe it was the right thing to do and that I believed in them. I then asked for their input.

One young lady raised her hand. "Can you read it to us for the first couple of chapters before giving us options? I think it would help us all get into the story?"

Other kids agreed. In fact, they all agreed. So, the plan changed before it even started.

"How are you grading us?"

Hey, they are ninth graders; they still don't fully understand my whole "numbers don't define you" thing just yet.

"We'll figure out some sort of project together at the end, just like the last literature unit. But, just like the last unit, no worksheets, quizzes, or tests. We are reading like human beings. We'll have some great discussions and learn how to actually read a book critically, but still enjoy it."

My honesty got them to buy in as well as get their thoughts about how we should proceed. The risk seems less to me after that conversation. The kids were with me. We were in it for the right reasons. And, we were able to move forward.

That risk produced some of the best, most far-reaching conversations I have had about literature in 21 years of teaching. Ninth graders were discussing topics like, "Do you have to change who you are in order to gain respect?" "Does love exist?" "Is art the only form of communication that is universal?" "How should someone fight against racism and discrimination?" "Is it really disrespectful to your family if you want to leave so you can better yourself?" And, we would discuss how Alexie formatted the book, his paragraphing, his word choice. We'd have genuine laughs together because we were all experiencing things at the same time. We would attempt those things in our writing, across all genres, from creative writing pieces, journal exercises, and even our argument writing.

The risk paid off with a meaningful unit. It wouldn't have happened if I hadn't been honest about my intentions and acknowledge that this was a risk. It focused the students, gave them some responsibility in the learning, and allowed for feedback. When things weren't going perfectly, students were comfortable enough to say so. And, because I had already been honest about not having all the answers, I was receptive to the feedback.

The funny thing about taking a risk is that if it is well reasoned, you never really get complaints. During that past unit, not one parent questioned why their kids were being taught this way. Not one administrator gave me the note to come and see them. From time to time, those things happen, but a well thought out, honest plan that is in the best interest of kids will always help show that the kids are being taught genuine skills that are exactly what the standards are asking for, but, more importantly, the skills that they need to be successful, productive, and happy human beings.

Be Willing to Be That Teacher

Kids talk. With social media, there are more avenues for them to talk. To be able to hide like I once did is really no longer an option. What you do in a room gets out there. Fast. This is something that all teachers need to get comfortable with. It isn't going away.

That's not to say that it doesn't make you feel uncomfortable. And, it shouldn't stop you from taking risks. If you want to make a difference for kids and give them a lesson that they won't forget, you must be willing to be the one who puts themselves out there.

I am comfortable being that guy and yet there are still times when I pause, just like that reading lesson. Early in September—in year 21—I was trying to come up with an idea to show kids that perspective in writing matters. Everything we read is truly a matter of perspective. It's a concept that is difficult to teach. I had brought in multiple accounts of the same issue—the news is full of that type of stuff—and I sensed that kids got it, but it wasn't real.

So, I came up with an idea. It was a risky idea because it involved me jumping out of the classroom window.

Ok, that sounds more dramatic than it really is because our classroom is on ground-level. The biggest risk would be that I could rip my pants on the window sill if I didn't hit the jump right.

The idea was that I would say I needed a pack of gum. I am known for always chewing gum, to the point where classes will buy me cases as gifts. After saying that, I would walk calmly to the back of the room, jump out the window, run to my car, get the gum, hop back in the window, and continue teaching.

I did just that. And, it worked out as intended. Kids were shocked. They were laughing when I came back in. We talked about what happened. I asked them to write about what happened. Most were done quickly. Then, we pushed to the next level. What happened inside the room? Who said what? What sounds were made? They worked longer. Their pieces were great, but varied.

One kid asked, "how can we have all saw the same thing, but have different versions?"

Boom. Magic. Risk worth it.

After class, a couple of colleagues asked why I was running the parking lot. I played it off and told them it was a writing lesson. But, later that night, my 10 year old daughter came up to me with a grin on her face.

"Dad, did you really jump out of the window in school today?"

I explained it all to her, but then it hit me. How did she know?

"Oh, it was on Instagram."

I'll admit that I was taken aback a bit. The thought of "did I risk too much?" ran through my head. That's normal, even for someone who is always willing to take a risk, let alone someone who has more fear. But, I grounded myself. The lesson was taught. The skills in the curriculum were the focus. And, my ninth graders got a vivid, meaningful experience. It was worth it. If I was ever called in for that lesson—I wasn't—I could definitely explain why it was best for kids. Notice I didn't say defend it. There isn't a defense. When you know that you are right and doing something for kids, you don't need to defend it. You only have to explain why.

Now, I don't recommend everyone jumping out of a window, but I do recommend you embracing the idea of doing something meaningful and impactful. You have to be willing to be that teacher who will get some looks from other colleagues and even get some Instagram views too.

Talk to Your Admin

You won't always get the answer you want, but that forces you to think better and to see things you wouldn't always see. There is generally a fear that comes with talking to your boss. It's normal. But, isolating yourself from your boss does a couple of things. First, it creates an aura of you doing something sneakily. It also doesn't allow you to collaborate. Whenever possible, speak to your principal, your assistant principal, or your department leader. Tell them about the "out of the box" idea you have. They may shoot it down. But, that doesn't mean it is a dead issue. It means you have to think more creatively and approach it differently.

Administrators see the whole picture. The really good administrators have the ability to see the small picture too, which is definitely the more important one. They know that your classroom lesson is the most important thing going on in their building. They will support your ideas if you have proven to be honest with them, willing to work with them, and willing to always put kids first. Even the strictest admin will help if you are consistent in your approach.

Set up a time to meet with them to explain your ideas. Show how it is a better approach for your kids to meet the curriculum. If your administrator is one who needs research rather than your word, come with the research. Make your case. If you believe that your innovation is better for kids, do everything you can to prove it to the administration.

Too much of my career was spent in the shadows, trying to hide my ideas from getting squashed. Had I been more honest and more willing to show what I was doing, I could have done even more innovative stuff. Over the past six years or so, I have been open. I've invited people in my classroom, I have gone to team teach with other teachers, and I talk with administrators openly about doing things differently. When I hit a roadblock, I look at it as an opportunity to make the idea better.

Be Willing to Fail

The true key to innovation and instructional risks is being willing to fail. That is scary to a lot of teachers. I get it; if you fail, you have 30 kids looking at you. You potentially have their parents questioning you. You could have admins or colleagues looking at you and wondering why you would fail rather than just go with what was done in the past.

And, there's the thing. Do we want to be stuck in the past and continue to give kids the same thing kids received 50 years ago? Is that safety—mediocrity—worth not preparing kids for their lives? Obviously, it isn't.

You have to be willing to fail.

And, if you are honest with kids, their parents, and administrators, even the failures can have successes. If your risks are rooted in the standards and are in the best interest of kids, failures will be at a minimum. And, even if there are failures, there will be enough gained to learn from them and do better the next time. Perhaps, even more importantly, kids will see that sometimes there is failure and that they will have to react and readjust. Isn't that a great lesson for them to see and hear?

A few years ago, I had what I thought was a pretty progressive idea. I was looking for a way to get my 11th graders to own their learning a bit more and to have more of an ability to individualize their learning. So, I decided that the third quarter would begin with a syllabus of everything they would be expected to accomplish. I gave them a book list, a bunch of different writing assignments, research work, and whatever else I would throw at them in 10 weeks. They would get that list and were allowed to work on it in whatever process or order they chose. If they felt like reading one day, could read. If they wanted to knock out their writing, they could. There were built in conferences for them to have with me so I thought it would be great.

Except, it wasn't. The kids did it and the work was accomplished. But, in my effort to get them to be independent, I lost a connection with them. And, because of the lack of structure, many had waited close to the end of the quarter to really get focused on work. That became my grading nightmare and the quality of conferences suffered. The idea was good, but it needed much more thought and structure. When I gave an end-of-unit evaluation, the kids were honest. They liked the concept, but they offered a bunch of alternative solutions. When the question was asked if they liked this setup, the overwhelming majority said no.

The idea was a flop. I knew it and they knew it. Yet, we learned from it. I learned that while kids appreciated the freedom, they needed a bit more of a focus and direction. They appreciated the freedom to explore topics and find ideas to write about, but freedom with everything was overwhelming. I hadn't thought of that. But, I wouldn't have known that unless I tried it out.

From that failure, I have learned to give kids freedom within one activity at a time. The writing process is their own and they work through it at their own pace. But, they aren't doing that and then having to juggle course reading. I help them along with that. My class still has more freedom than most, but it is focused on one, maybe two tasks at a time. Without taking that risk a few years ago and learning from failure, I would not be the teacher I am today.

Was it embarrassing and did I feel bad when we failed? Sure. But, I knew I was doing it for the right reasons. I knew the concept was good. I believed in it. Kids knew why. Parents knew why. My administrators knew why. While the idea wasn't a success, there was not one complaint at all. In fact, at parent-teacher conferences, many parents complimented me on letting their kids see what college could look like. They appreciated a different approach and that it led to their kid actually liking English class.

So, yes, it was a failure, but even in failure, I grew because I evolved, adjusted, and did better the next time. I didn't revert back to "what we always did". I continued to push forward. There will be times when we fail. But, I would rather fail in trying to do something great for kids than coast and being mediocre.

And, that's the word that seems like a perfect landing spot for this chapter. Nobody aspires to be mediocre. We don't want our own children to be mediocre. We don't want our students to be mediocre. Why would we want to teach like a mediocre teacher? Kids know when they are stuck with mediocrity. It's one of the reasons they dislike school.

We need to be innovative. We need to take those risks, openly and honestly. We need to involve our students, parents, and our administrators in those risks. If we do, the magic moments will happen. Those moments are worth the occasional failures.

Innovative Risk Takeaways for Admins

→ Be the one who helps your teachers figure out how to try all of their ideas no matter how outlandish.

→ When teachers take risks and fail, pick them up and encourage them to try again.

→ Motivation decreases and boredom increases as kids progress through school. That is on us; let's try to fix that.

→ Model a different approach to teaching during your faculty meetings and PD sessions.

→ Encourage teachers to give students a cause to promote, a problem to solve, or better yet ask them what problem they want to solve and then help them to solve it!

→ Support the use of social media, it is a great place for teachers to find and share great ideas.

→ Give permission for your teachers to "break the rules" if it benefits students.

→ Ask teachers how you can help them to be more creative.

→ Remember not everyone has the same strengths or passions; teaching is an art. Administrators should encourage teachers to be who they are rather than carbon copies of what we think they should be.

→ Let school be fun! Give up some control.

Innovative Risk Takeaways for Teachers

→ The traditional belief that education is the great equalizer is true. We must break every other tradition in education so that education can be an equalizer for today's kids in today's world.

→ If a lesson is rooted in the standards, content can and should be engaging to kids.

→ An innovative teacher must be honest with kids about taking a risk. The goals of the lesson and the reason for the risk must be transparent.

→ An innovative teacher must be willing to withstand the pressure to conform. The more you deviate from what has always been done, the more the pressure will be there to conform.

→ An innovative teacher must be willing to fail and learn from that failure. Often, it provides even more meaningful life lessons for kids and makes a teacher better in the long term.

→ An innovative teacher must be willing to talk to their administrator and be open about the intentions of the new approach.

→ An innovative teacher must be willing to listen to student feedback and adjust accordingly. It's not the idea that is important; the only important thing is student learning.

→ Innovation can be scary. Find like-minded educators to share ideas with and to encourage the risk that will be beneficial to students.

VOICES FROM THE FIELD...
By Shelly Sanchez Terrell

One of the most famous innovators is Thomas Edison. Edison became famous for his many inventions, including the light bulb. The light bulb made life safer and easier for people around the world. Edison designed over 10,000 prototypes of the light bulb before coming up with the design he patented. What makes Edison a notable innovator is not necessarily his inventions, but his drive and determination to revise his original idea several times till he came up with the right solution. If Edison would have given up after one of the thousands of failed prototypes, then the world would be a much darker place.

Innovators solve problems and improve the quality of life for many. Innovation is also a long journey filled with many failed designs that need reflection and revision. So many bright young minds quit after the first time they face obstacles or what they think of as failure.

In order to help more bright young minds blossom and develop perseverance, schools must involve students in the process of innovation throughout their learning journeys. The curricula and learning environment must offer students enough opportunities to design solutions to problems they care about. Schools need to help students believe they have the power to transform the world by providing learners with opportunities to make a difference in their communities. Makerspaces, coding, problem/project based learning, robotics, 3D printing, STEAM programs, contests, global collaboration projects, experiments, and field research are some ways that schools can involve students in the process of innovation.

Additionally, teachers and the community need to champion student imagination and creativity. Student ideas, innovations, creations and imaginations need to be announced and publicized. When learners walk in the building they should see their ideas celebrated and displayed so they feel empowered to continue striving to improve the world.

8

Mindfulness and Supporting Students

We can set up schools with all of our best practices. We can establish an excellent teacher and admin team. We can involve parents and do all of the things to make our field more relevant and more engaging. All of that is important.

But, all of that doesn't mean a thing if we don't establish an environment where our kids are valued, respected, and treated well. We must not only acknowledge kids' individuality, stressors, and passions, we must value them. We must do everything to make kids feel safe in school. If we can do that, schools can be that magical place kids deserve.

An administrator must model that behavior with their staff. A good administrator realizes that teachers need their own mindfulness training and awareness and must provide opportunities for them to practice that skill. If an administrator truly values the teacher as a human being, can help in times of trouble, and can allow for professional opportunities for teachers to learn new calming techniques and coping mechanisms, the teacher will be better in the classroom. More importantly, the teacher will be better for kids.

A teacher must set an environment that values each kid. A good teacher shows that each kid matters, their voice matters, and their overall happiness matters. Teachers must be willing to be there for kids beyond the curricular demands. When a teacher truly values a student for who they are, a student not only performs better in the classroom, but is a calmer, more confident person who cannot only thrive, but know how to deal with stressful situations.

The Admin

"Close your eyes for a moment. Now, picture a young person you care greatly for. It can be your child, grandchild, a niece, a nephew, or any young person who touched your heart. Now, think about what you want for them when they are 25 to 30 years old. Pick three or four words to describe them in this ideal state at that age."

Marc Brackett, the founder of the Yale Center for Emotional Intelligence and lead developer for R.U.L.E.R, a systematic and evidence-based approach to social and emotional learning, posed this question to a room full of educators. The responses were pretty consistent:

- » Happy
- » Healthy
- » Good Person
- » Content
- » Fulfilled

Dr. Brackett then asked a rhetorical, yet important question.

"If these qualities are so important, if they are what we want for our young people, how come we spend such little time developing these qualities in schools?"

That statement is one that has stayed with me for a long time. In fact, I have used his exercise several times in various sessions I have led.

176

It seems so obvious when we take a step back. We want students who are happy, healthy, good people. We want to develop citizens who contribute to society and who are fulfilled with the work they do, the contributions they make. Yet, we rarely teach these things in schools; in fact, there can be a stigma that comes with placing too much value on these "soft skills" in our schools.

How can teachers be expected to get through the dense curriculum and still take time for, as some jaded teachers may say, the "cumbia stuff"?

Mindfulness, although becoming more mainstream of late, still makes some people uncomfortable. Restorative practices can be perceived as "soft on crime". Reflection rooms are still seen as a place where children should be consequenced rather than prepared to learn. I can certainly understand this sentiment. Teachers have a great deal of pressure on them from outside forces to deliver curriculum, to deliver glowing test scores. Principals are responsible for overseeing a building that is a safe, orderly institution for learning. It is scary to try a different approach, to lessen punishments, and increase instructional practices on empathy, respect, behavior.

Things can quickly get out of control when order is not maintained, negatively affecting those students who are, in fact, ready to learn. The problem is what we are currently doing is not working. Things are not getting better.

We have more resources, technologies that are supposed to make life more convenient and easier to figure out. The problem is things seem to be speeding up, stressing up, and none of us seem to be able to keep up as the treadmill of life keeps getting faster and faster.

There is some startling evidence that we need to do better with taking care of our kids' mental health and our own for that matter.

There were 307 Mass Shootings in 2018, 40 of which occurred in schools.

Teen Suicide rates went up over 70% from 2006-2016.

In a recent poll of 10s of Thousands High School Students, 45% of the students said they were stressed all the time.

177

50% of teenagers have misused drugs.

Each generation claims its hardships to the one after it, laying claim to a more difficult, challenging life. It is one where kids were expected to do more and do with less, and, until recently, these claims have, more times than not, been justified.

Things progress, our society progresses, and, as we advance as a people, the natural progression is that things get easier. We have more time for leisure, more time for thought, more time to connect with others. It is more time to spend on bigger things and less on mundane tasks.

Unfortunately, it seems we have reached a tipping point. The exponential advancement of technology has put our youth in a unique situation, one that is difficult for adults to understand.

A hyper-connected society that expects superficial interaction at the expense of true connection. A fast-paced world that leaves less and less time for deep work, less and less time for contemplation and reflection.

With the world literally at their fingertips, they can create anything, connect with anyone, be heard by the masses. It certainly has exciting prospects, but not without a cost.

Our children do not know how to handle these new found freedoms and powers. It is not that they are lazy, or bored, or rude, or obnoxious; it is that they are struggling to keep their heads above water in a world where so much is possible and so much is expected.

How do we, a generation that did not have to navigate the burden of these advancements, help today's youth navigate these new and ever-changing realities of this next revolution?

I certainly do not claim to have all of the answers, but I do know that putting our heads in the sand and using the same techniques that obviously are not working any longer is not the answer. Blaming this generation and pointing to their shortfalls does nothing to solve the problem we are facing and, more importantly, our kids are facing. It is a new world and it is our job to help them navigate this new reality.

The question is how do we do it? Certainly not by continuing to do what we have always done. A new world calls for new strategies.

One of the initiatives I am most proud of in our District is our Kaleidoscope Team at West Haverstraw Elementary School. This team takes a different approach with students who struggle behaviorally and academically.

The principal of the school, Mary Esposito, came to me one day concerned about several students in grades 1 and 2 who she feared were not performing on grade level, struggling behaviorally, and in danger of being retained or classified.

"We need to do something different. I can't do another year of the same old, same old and watch these kids flounder."

The frustration in her voice was apparent, but with this principal, as with the best leaders, when she presents a problem, she also offers a solution.

Mary was lucky to have a teacher, Reyna Texler (AKA Ruby Sneakers), who is what I would call a school mindfulness expert and a child whisperer working in her building. They worked together to devise a plan, a different approach. Thus, the Kaleidoscope Team was born.

Basically, the 20 or so most challenging students in grades 1 and 2 were placed in cohorts - four, first and second grade classes. Reyna was placed on special assignment as an intervention specialist who pushed into these classes working with the students in small groups. Her focus while working with these students was primarily to provide them with strategies to recognize their emotions, observe those emotions, and avoid having those emotions dictate the decisions they made throughout their day.

Breathing strategies, mindfulness exercises, and emotional intelligence activities are all incorporated into the work she does with our kids. The self-awareness work is often done through content, but the primary goal is always their mental well-being.

In lieu of the push-in reading teacher, the team was additionally supported by an AIS teacher who focused on foundational ELA and Math skills and two teaching assistants. The cost of the support was through title funds, which, in essence, amounted to one teacher and one teacher's assistant since the reading teacher's caseload working with the four classes was comparable to what it would be without this program.

Since the program is in its infancy, hard data on its effectiveness is limited. That being said, the anecdotal evidence of success is strong. Plus, I am not convinced that the positive impact this program does or doesn't have can be measured with the ambiguous data we use to measure success in schools. In fact, I am not convinced the data we currently use is as informative or useful as we have been led to believe in the field of education over the last 15 years, years in which terms like "data-driven" "measurable results" and "adequate progress" etc. were born.

When I see a first grade child teaching one of his classmates strategies for dealing with anxiety during a high wind storm, I know it is working. I have hope for our field as we begin to see teaching kids how to cope with their emotions, teaching kids how to interact with others, teaching them how to deal with trauma, how teaching kids these skills is no longer just beneficial, it is essential.

How do we make teaching students social-emotional skills, practicing presence, and prioritizing mental and emotional well-being the norm and just the way we do business in school?

I long for the days when all the adults in a school building see their students, truly see them, see them for the raw, emotional, ever changing, ever struggling, self-conscious individuals they are.

I long for the days when all adults in a school building are most concerned with guiding their students through this critical point in their lives compassionately. School's first priority is to help students first to survive the poverty, violence, insecurity, anger, sadness, highs, and lows to make it to adulthood a well-adjusted happy person, despite all the obstacles children face.

I long for the days when schools are more concerned with the mental skills kids need for success in life than the facts, figures, algorithms, and analysis that our political stalwarts deem as an essential and equitable educational program.

I long for the days when we put kids before curriculum.

Yet, like anything else, we can complain, but as Teddy Roosevelt was quoted as saying, "Complaining without proposing a solution is whining."

So the question becomes: what can we do? What small steps can we take to start improving our schools so they meet not only the academic needs of our students, but their developmental, social, emotional needs as well?

The first step is taking care of ourselves. We cannot be as compassionate, caring, and effective if we are not in a good place emotionally, if we are overstressed.

Consider developing the following habits:

Meditation
Meditation is certainly in vogue right now and that sometimes can lead to a backlash. I would suggest judging for yourself. I have found that when I meditate consistently I am kinder, happier, and more efficient. I would suggest keeping it simple. I use the Headspace APP, which offers various guided meditation exercises. Start small and try the three-minute sessions for a week. I have worked my way up to 10-minute sessions on most days, but I find benefits even when I take just a minute to meditate before coming to work or before entering a tough meeting.

Journal
Again, simplicity is the key. 3-5 minutes in the morning can produce results that will not only help your mental state, but will help you to prioritize and set intentions for your day. A simple template you could follow:

» One thing I am grateful for at home...

» The best part of my day yesterday was...

» One student I want to connect with today...

» One adult I want to connect with today...

» One thing I will do to be healthy today...

» One thing I want to accomplish at work...

» One thing I want to do for fun today...

» One thing I will do today to grow as a professional...

» One thing I will do to grow as a person today...

Go Out to Lunch

Commit to going out to lunch at least one day each week. Too often, educators shovel their food in their mouths as they make lesson plans, counsel kids, or grade papers. It is not unreasonable to break bread with a friend out of your place of work in a nice environment at least once a week.

Chunk Your Tens

I love using a timer to accomplish things I want to accomplish or to take care of myself. Setting a timer to read for ten minutes, write for ten minutes, rest for ten minutes, go for a walk for ten minutes, or whatever you decide to do can have a transformative effect on your peace of mind, as well as your sense of accomplishment.

How many times have you wasted those 10 minutes before your next class, meeting, or event playing on Facebook, sifting through emails, or buying things you don't really need on Amazon? Those ten-minute blocks can lead to so many things you would never have imagined possible. Heck, without chunking my tens, this book probably would never have been written.

Notice

Reyna Texler taught me a trick that I have applied on certain days and even expanded upon. She told me as she walked into her school for the day she tried to notice as many sounds as she could before the door of the building shut behind her. I love doing this activity as well as taking days to notice. I have played this game on certain days by noticing:

- Christmas lights.
- As many different types of flowers as I can.
- Eagles I can find in a week.
- People who may need a pick me up.

Consider embedding the following tchniques in your classrooms:

Break Areas

Establish a location in your room where students can self-direct themselves to go to when they need to. These locations can have glitter jars, calming scripts, headphones with sap music, positive affirmation cards, or whatever you and your students decide they need to help them regulate their emotions. Practice with students when they should go to these areas, and how they can be in that space without disrupting others.

I know this practice may scare some teachers who will think that students will take advantage of this area and never pay attention to academics in their classes. I would ask, isn't this a better solution for the students who consistently distract your classes and are sent to the office? The optimist in me would like to think kids will use this tool appropriately and ultimately improve the classroom environment for all.

Breathing Exercises

1. 4 Square Breathing - Students trace a square on their hand. Up breathing in, to a count of four, across, hold for four, down, out to a count of four, across, to a count of four. Repeat four times.
2. Hand Trace - Breathe in as you trace up your finger, out as you trace down. Continue through all of your fingers and then repeat in the other direction.
3. Three Breath - Commit to stopping three times every day and take three breaths. Focus only on your breath and your surroundings. Try to be present rather than thinking about what you need to do.

Silent Reflection Time

When facilitating sessions for adults, or students for that matter, I often find myself trying to get as much "in" as I can. I now realize the importance of processing what we hear, what we learn. It is not how much we "cover." Rather,

183

it is how much our learners actually learn and understand. I have begun asking participants to sit silently and reflect on a question or information presented rather than immediately talking about, writing about, or doing something with the content. The first thing we have noticed is that two minutes of silence in a room of 30 people seems like a long time! We are now noticing how effective this brief amount of time to reflect on our learning.

Gratitude
Take a minute or two each day to practice gratitude. This can be facilitated by teachers in the classroom, over the morning announcements, or as part of a learning center. Giving a gratitude topic of the day (food, nature, people, smells, books, movies etc..) can help to get students started. The research behind the benefits of expressing gratitude is undeniable. The time spent seems to be well worth it.

Notice Walks
Going on a "notice" walk can be an excellent way to practice mindfulness, increase creative thinking, and build learning connections. Take your class, your faculty, your principals on a notice walk. These walks should be silent expeditions around the school, on the grounds, or simply around the room. Direct them to notice things such as interactions between people, how trees grow, how many colors they can see in the hallways, the oldest object they can find, or whatever else you can think of that will support learning.

Dark Listening
Read to your students and ask them to close their eyes while you read. I first saw this done by a principal as he read a passage from a professional book to his staff. I experienced it with the faculty and noticed how much more engaged with the text I was with my eyes closed. I have since used it in PD sessions and have been happy with the reaction and engagement I have been getting from the participants. School and District Leaders Consider modeling the practices in PD sessions and faculty meetings that you would like to see teachers embed in their classrooms.

Explore New Courses and Schedules
There are always restraints on what we can do because of State requirements, union contracts, and monetary issues. That hasn't stopped some excellent

leaders I know from getting creative and adding advisory programs, STEM labs, mindfulness rooms, Emotional Intelligence initiatives, and after-school clubs. The best leaders use the resources they have, find ways to cut the red tape, and take chances because they believe in the emotional health and wellness of their students just as much as they care about their academic well being.

Get the School Involved

Get your school involved with activities such as Global School Play Day, March Forward, Mix it Up Day to name a few. Family wellness nights, school assemblies, or spontaneous acts like passing out ice pops on a hot day, or ringing the bell and announcing recess for all (just make sure you let your teachers know ahead of time) are just some ways to get the whole community involved.

Listen to Your People

The greatest resource we have as administrators is the people we work with. Listen to their great ideas and even the ones that seem not so great. Be willing to take a chance on them, be willing to support those ideas, be willing to make school fun!

A program is not going to solve the crisis our students are facing in regards to their mental health, but caring, aware adults recognizing that we must adjust to our students' needs will help us shift culture, ultimately improving not only the state of mind of our students, but their ability to learn as well.

The Teacher

The drive for us to change education and our practices all comes down to one thing that we have repeated quite a bit throughout these pages. This desire to change is to make schools a better place for kids. This isn't about being soft or lowering expectations. It is about treating kids with dignity, treating them with respect, taking the time to learn how they learn, and see them as more than just a student. They are a human being with the same needs, desires, fears, need to belong, insecurities, passions, and everything else that we, the adults, wake up with.

Everything in this book has led to this chapter. And, we have left this chapter as the finale because this is why we, along with so many others, are in the fight for improving and evolving our schools. Our kids need us to be that person. We need to not only teach them the skills from our content areas so that they can be competent workers and offer skills to the outside world. We must also teach and model for them how to be good citizens now, at their age, and in the future. We must teach them that their words, their voice, their skills have the capability to change the world now and in the future. We must teach them that failure happens and it is never an end. We must teach them that grief enters our life and we can deal with it in a healthy way. We must teach them that we can deal with stress and learn what types of stress are truly dangerous. We must teach that it is alright to pursue a passion and that the happiest adults are actually the ones who are working with their passions. We must teach them that they are not a number. We must teach them that they matter.

That's a pretty big "we must" list, isn't it?

I probably missed quite a few as well. The point is that our job as classroom teachers is always beyond the curriculum. It is beyond grades, homework, and even skills. Our job is to help raise people.

Some—the naysayers—will scoff at that. And, that's ok. As we have seen throughout history and even in our story about improving education, those who challenge the convention are always challenged and portrayed as soft. We must rise above that; we must mute the naysayers and relegate them to a spot in the corner where they begin to feel obsolete. Maybe they will change; that would be great. Or, maybe they will fade away into oblivion. Either way, education will improve.

The term used today is Social Emotional Learning. I like that it has a name and that it is being put out there on a worldwide front. Honestly, it is just a fancy way of saying treating kids well. So, how do you go about treating kids well? The first place to start is to own it. When you own it and become known as someone who puts kids first, you will get your fair share of naysayer pressure.

In my office, I have this sign that states a list of things about being there for kids. It's basically a promise to listen and value kids and that they are the reason I am here. It was made for me by one of my colleagues, someone who is often chastised for putting kids first. I have it proudly in my office, hanging amongst my baseball memorabilia.

One day, a naysayer walks in. He stands there, reading the sign. "Damn, Gary. You are really drinking the Kool Aid, aren't?"

I know what he means, but I want to make this difficult for him. In the past, I would've laughed and said something to the effect that it's no big deal. But, I own who I am and what I can do for kids.

I don't even look up from my computer, "What do you mean?"

"This sign? Really?"

Again, I don't look up.

"Oh, you mean a sign that shows I actually give a f**k about kids and take this job seriously? You mean the sign that perfectly says exactly why I am here? If it is funny, that's great. But, I actually like kids and love this job."

He walked out without saying a word. He never came back into my office and it took him a good couple of months to even look me in the eye when we passed in the hallway.

Later that month, I had an encounter with another colleague who I have so much respect for in the classroom. The knowledge, depth, and creativity are second to none. This colleague gave me an email exchange between them and a kid. I had taught the kid the previous year so I knew that he was a hardworking young man with a lot going on. The kid wrote the teacher, sort of venting about keeping up and that he was surprised that there was suddenly a test. The teacher wrote back a pretty scathing response, basically saying to "suck it up" and drop the course if it was too much. I was forwarded the email with a "could you believe this kid?" I wish I didn't see that because, as the Department Coordinator and someone who cares about the field, I knew this was wrong. No kid should receive an email like that. So, the next day, I stopped up and my colleague came to the hallway.

"Did you see that email? Can you believe that he said that?"

"I know you aren't going to like this, but you're wrong. What you said and how you said it was wrong. Here was a kid reaching out to you and you essentially told him to shut the hell up."

That didn't go over very well.

"No, I am preparing him for college when the professors don't care. He chose to take this class and do all of his other stuff. Who is he to challenge me?"

"He wasn't challenging you. He was venting about having a lot of work, something new added on. He was looking for some guidance. He isn't the type of kid to pop off or be disrespectful. He was looking for help. That's why we are here. We are here to help kids learn how to deal."

"You know, you are way too soft on kids."

I think my look stopped the conversation. I had a smirk and started to walk away, but I didn't turn around.

Then, I stopped.

It was time to own it.

"Thank you."

Now, there was a new look of disbelief because I wasn't angry at all.

"If being too soft means that I care about kids, well then I am ok with it. You just gave me a huge compliment. I am doing something right. I know you are better than what you wrote in your email. I've seen it. That wasn't your finest moment, but it's ok. I know you're better than that."

I owned it. It's difficult to have those conversations, especially with people you do have respect for. And, while the teacher went back into the room and told the class that I didn't want students to do any work and that I was too soft on skills, the conversation still drives me to this day. We can do better for kids. We can teach them skills, have really high expectations for them, and challenge them without tearing them down. These are not mutually exclusive things.

We can make schools challenging, enriching, and impactful and really set kids up to use their talents now and in the future. We can do all of that without driving them to the point of breakdown, stress, or sleeplessness. We can have all of that challenge and have a happy, healthy, well-rounded kids. We just have to evolve.

Workload

There is no doubt that we have to prepare kids differently than we did even 10 years ago, let alone 30 or 40 years ago. In a complex world, we must develop those complex skills so that kids can find their path. But, we, as an industry, have gotten far off track. In this whole race to get kids to reach their potential, the focus has shifted to what's next. In elementary school, it is about getting prepared for Middle School. In Middle School, it's about being ready for High School. And, of course, then it becomes about College.

In that race to prepare and win in that system, schools are offering more advanced level courses than ever before. We now have sophomores with nearly full college loads at the age of 15. Honors programs have expanded as well. Many schools are now offering academies, which allows students to explore areas in greater depth.

That's the key term: depth. We mistake the word depth for the word more. In our race to prepare kids, the education industry has given more. More classes. More work. More tests. More homework. Just more. And, what has that created? It has created a group of kids who are more stressed out than at any other point in our history. And, where is the data that the current system is better preparing them for anything? Like we discussed in our grading chapter, all we are doing with this concept of more is creating a game of school. Kids are smart enough to survive so they will find ways to divide and conquer. They will cut through the stuff that isn't attached to the number so they can survive. They sleep less. They come to class tired and overwhelmed. And, they lose the true purpose of school: to develop a love of learning and to find a passion. That's why they are there. But, we push that message away.

More is not better. Having a middle school student in an honors program spend five or six hours of homework is not better. It is not academically sound and it is not good for their well being.

We must break from the tradition and parse carefully through our curriculum and figure out what is essential. What are the skills that kids need to learn? Then, we must pick the content to best teach those skills. And, finally, we must measure how much of that will allow students to balance their learning, their passions, and their outside interests. If we want to turn out well-rounded kids, we must develop them to be well rounded, not to have them spend hours and hours on an assignment that is often rooted in compliance and rote skills.

For my classes, we focus on a particular writing skill. We'll spend time in class working through that process. We conference daily. We work on revising and editing. Once it is done, they are allowed redos. There is no stress of a grade. There is only the focus on learning. With reading, we try to find things we are all interested in. And, even if we are reading something difficult, we are working on the skill together and then they work in pairs, and then independently. We are working on higher level skills in a purposeful manner. Kids know that I am not looking to get them.

That can be done in every classroom, in every curricular area. Math classes can give specific problems and options to work through, rather than a voluminous, one size fits all assignment. Social Studies can accomplish curricular skill goals without six-hour long outline assignments. Again, this isn't softening or diluting expectations. It is about targeting those expectations so kids know that it is important to learn, but that they will also have time to enjoy other interests, much like we have as adults. If we want to pass along life long skills, we must teach them those life long skills, not cram these lessons and assignments that take an inordinate amount of time and quell any sort of passion, while heightening anxiety.

We must be purposeful. We must be mindful of the work we give. More is not better. Quality is better. Passion driven is better. Relevant is better.

If we can keep those things in mind, our students will be more driven, more purposeful, more willing to try, and more willing to continue after the first blockade to success.

Classroom Management

If there is one area that receives little to no attention when it comes to teacher training, it is classroom management. It is sometimes called discipline, but that word has such negative connotations. Discipline means that something went wrong and that we have to dole out punishment. And, as much as this is going to make some readers cringe, discipline is largely the failing of the teacher. Sure, there are times when kids will misbehave for no reason, but those are few and far between. The fact is that if we manage our room correctly and truly listen to kids, we can avoid those discipline situations.

My first year of teaching was a challenge; every first-year teacher finds that year challenging. I was finding my way through being the guy in front of the room, but nothing prepared me for managing a class. Before I even stepped foot in my own class, I had attended the welcome meeting for new teachers. We would tour the district, hear about all of the great things, and then hear from our Union. Each building representative would meet with us and talk about how to conduct yourself as a professional. Discipline was a topic. The message: don't take any crap. Show them who's boss. Do it early and you'll save yourself a lot of headache.

I was never any good at that. I tried it out during my first and second years of teaching. But, it just wasn't me. I was better at talking to kids and trying to get to the root of the problem. I didn't know it then, but I was developing my attitude of "there is always a reason". Kids always have a reason for their behavior. Heck, even adults have a reason when they don't perform at their jobs after years of steady performance. It may sound Pollyanna, but kids aren't coming to school hoping to get in trouble. And, if they aren't interested in the work, there is a reason.

That's where management comes in. One of the first things that I would encourage all teachers is to keep a notebook of your kids. I do this for a couple of reasons. First, I use it to take notes on our writing conversations. But, I also jot down little things that I could use later on. I jot down things that they like or things that they may say, and things I noticed. A lot of the time, I don't need to look at this, but it is helpful to have those notes.

Aside from that, management is really dependent upon the group of kids in front of you. That's why anyone telling you there is a key or a specific method of classroom management isn't being honest. Like instruction, how can a one size fits all discipline plan ever work? Kids are different. Each one brings a different set of circumstances. You have to deal with things individually.

My style of management is open and based on the individual. It has evolved over my career and it looks slightly different each year. Again, it depends on the group in front of you. I don't even hand out class rules anymore. Instead, I talk about respect and how I will earn their respect. They automatically get mine. I acknowledge that they have a difficult job and I respect the task in front of them. I promise to work with them and do whatever I can to be there for them. That approach generally gets buy-in. Of course, there are some who will test it. When that happens, it is time to figure out why.

Management is never done in front of the class. You never shame a kid in front of an audience, ever. Even if a kid is "making you look bad" in front of the class, you must be the one to ride out the storm and then have a talk. The talk should always start with, "What's up? How can I help you?" When I start with those two questions, even the angriest of kids immediately calm down. They see that I actually care and don't want to just punish them. They may protest a little longer, but it generally ends with tears filling their eyes—yes, high school kids cry—and the reason comes out. That opens a door for a conversation, most likely multiple conversations. Whether it is a problem with peers, at home, or pressures from school, the reason comes out. Then, you form a relationship and a plan. Generally, those behavior issues go away.

With those relationships being formed, you will also learn something Rick Wormeli wrote, "Fair Is Not Always Equal." To successfully manage a class, there are most likely 30 sets of rules, one for each person. Many teachers are afraid of this because of the fear of standing out or a lack of uniformity. Plus, it flies in the face of the tradition of order and rules written on a schoolhouse chalkboard. But, it is the only way to get kids to buy in.

This was put to the test one year when I was asked to do some model teaching with a group of seventh graders. They were a great, eager bunch of kids. But, on the first day, I noticed a young man just sitting quietly in his seat, reading a book from the library. Unlike the rest of the class, he wasn't engaged in our argument lesson. The commercials, the "homework sucks" chants failed to get him.

His teacher was a bit upset and expressed that it was an issue all year. I asked if the team had asked why. They had asked guidance, but didn't find an answer. I wanted to dig. The next day, I approached him quietly and asked him what he was reading. He was hesitant, but told me a little about the book. He asked if he had to put it away. I said no, but try to keep an ear out for me when we were doing the argument stuff.

It wasn't fair to the rest of the kids, but it worked. The kid read, but gradually started to engage. When I pushed a bit a week later, he withdrew back to the book. I started to ask guidance and the principal about him. I found out the reason. He had been through something horrific at home. It is something no kid should ever have to endure. So, there was a reason. When I told his team of teachers, their attitudes towards his aloofness changed. He was a kid in need of help and would not be able to conform to one set of rules like everyone else. While his work wasn't perfect, I was able to at least get him to give me some writing to work with. And, every once in a while, he would smile.

You manage to the kid, not to one set of rules.

Of course, every school has a code of conduct and a referral system. Those are things that should be last resort things, saved for only serious offenses. Teachers who become too reliant on the discipline system and begin to write referrals for behaviors that could be worked on individually, lose all control of the class. You are giving the message that you can't handle things on your own. The same goes for when you call an administrator in to talk to the class. It says you can't handle it and that you don't value your relationship with the student. If you take the time to form a relationship with kids, work at that relationship, leave them with their dignity when it comes to addressing behaviors, and always work to find the reason behind the behavior, you will set a positive classroom environment that is stress-free and fear free. If you do that, you will have created a relationship with each kid and you won't even know what a school referral looks like.

When kids know that they are in an environment where they won't be embarrassed and they are allowed to make mistakes, they are comfortable, they know they are valued, and they will be at their best to learn.

Being There

The job of a teacher is more than just curriculum. It is about being there for a kid in any way that they need. Whether it is being available to talk with a kid, offer extra help, or just spend five minutes talking about something other than class, it makes a big difference. Think about it. Nobody wants to come to work where they aren't valued or seen as a human being. We chastise our bosses if they don't try to get to know us or hide in their offices. Why would we do the same thing to kids?

Being there doesn't always require a lot of time. In my younger days, I was able to show up at all of the sporting events and school functions to see my kids outside of the classroom. It was easy. But, as I aged and had my daughter, that time, rightfully, was spent with her. But, there are still ways to show that I am there for them.

Make a point to be in the hallways and take that minute to say hi to kids. Talk with them. Ask how their events went. Kids just want to know that you are interested and care. Make it a point to have lunch with them sometime. One veteran teacher from my early years always had lunch in the student cafeteria. He would sit with kids, talk with them, and really listen to them.

Now, that doesn't mean you should give up your lunch every day or anything. We need time to recharge too. But, having lunch once in a while with kids is a good way to connect. My daughter's fourth grade teacher had this as a prize every week with her class. All of the kids in her class were excited when they had the opportunity to pick that prize. Spending time with kids is the best acknowledgement that they matter. When they know that they matter, they will want to work. Make time for those conversations. They are more important and more memorable than any lesson you teach.

Think about it. Who was your favorite teacher? Why were they your favorite? I bet the first 10 reasons have nothing to do with the content they taught you. It was because they were there for you and took the time to know you and help you with life. Be that for a kid.

It Truly is the Little Things

And, that is exactly what it comes down to. It is the little moments that we share with kids each day that become the fabric of their humanity, the reason for why they pursue things, or the courage they summon to be who they are and chase their dreams. It is about us greeting them at the door as they come in. It's about us learning about their interests, the jokes in class, the conversations in passing. Yes, it is about being there for the big moments and those life talk moments. But, those don't happen without the little moments.

We matter in kids' lives. Of course, we are there to teach our subject matter. But, we are there to help form happy, healthy human beings. A kind word, an email, or taking the extra minute to listen to a kid can make all the difference. If we treat kids with dignity, get to know them, treat them as individuals, and keep the focus on their development, kids will look forward to class. More importantly, we will not only arm them with the skills to make a difference in the world, but we will develop content, secure people who will have the confidence to make a difference in the world.

How to Treat Kids Takeaways for Admins

→   Doing the same thing we have always done to improve student behavior is not working.

→   A recent poll found that 45% of students are stressed all the time.

→   Students need help navigating the pressures they are under.

→   Put kids' mental health before curriculum.

→   In order to help our students with their mental health, we need to take care of our own mental health.

→   Strategies to help students mental health can be built into existing curriculum.

→   Try to start your day with meditation and/or journaling.

→   Plan for your own self-care.

→   Model strategies with teachers and students.

→   Practice gratitude.

How To Treat Kids Takeaways for Teachers

→   Bottom line, a teacher's job is to provide an environment where kids feel valued and can be open and honest.

→   You must be willing to "own" your mission to value kids. There will be naysayers.

→   Teachers must be mindful of a students' workload. Your class isn't the only thing in their lives. We must encourage passions.

→   More is not better when it comes to education. If we cram more, we heighten anxiety in our students.

→   We must be purposeful with the work we give students.

→   There is always a reason for student behavior.

→   Classroom management looks different for each kid.

→   The key to management is to establish a genuine relationship.

→   Show a kid that you care about them more than just as a student in your class. They are a person. They matter.

→   The little moments each day are what makes our connection with kids strong.

VOICES FROM THE FIELD...

Reyna Texler, Ruby Sneakers Consulting LLC

If you're looking for best practices on how to treat children, look into the eyes of a child. Look beyond the beautiful blues, the vibrant hazels, the deep browns, and the many shades in between. Look beyond what level they're currently reading at, how fluently they know their math facts, or whether or not they've mastered the writing skills the class is currently focusing on.

Each child brings their unique story with them to school each day. When you look into the eyes of a child, look deep into their hearts. See their fears, their desire to feel safe physically, socially, and emotionally. When we make the health and well-being of our children a priority, we empower them with the core skills necessary to make a positive impact on the world.

Listen to their need to have their voice heard and their thoughts and feelings validated. See their desire for a space, free of judgement, filled with support, and your full presence even though the deadline of a scope and sequence is calling. Create an environment where all emotions are welcomed and emotional intelligence is strengthened. Once a child's social-emotional needs are met, their opportunity for academic success begins to soar.

Look beyond labeling behaviors as defiance, and reframe them as their only form of communication until you're able to teach them the skills and tools they need to overcome their problems. Restorative practices open the doorway to change by modeling collaboration, empathy and compassion as you work through solving problems with them.

One of the greatest influences on a child's social, emotional, and cognitive development is the presence of a relationship that provides unconditional love. For some children, school may be the one place they feel this strongest emotion. For some children, you may be the one person who shows them what love means.

The words a child hears shapes the world in which they live in. We have the ability to change the trajectory of how students perceive themselves.

Acting with compassion should be our standard for not only children, but everyone we encounter on a daily basis. We have the ability to bring out the best in everyone. So, just in case you haven't heard it today...

You are seen.
You are loved.
You are appreciated.
Thank you for being an incredible educator helping to change the world.

ABOUT THE AUTHORS

Dr. Kris Felicello has been in the field of education for over 25 years as a Teacher, Coach, Athletic Director, Assistant Principal, Principal, Assistant Superintendent of Human Resources, and he is currently the Assistant Superintendent of Educational Services in the North Rockland Central School District in Rockland County, New York. Kris obtained his Doctor of Education degree in Educational Leadership from St. John's University in 2011.

Dr. Felicello is leader who wants to make schools a better place for students. He firmly believes that it is essential to build relationships and foster students' social-emotional development to ensure a positive and productive educational experience for all students. Throughout his career, Dr. Felicello has embraced technology as a means to improve schools, however he cautions that technology should be utilized only when it supports positive instructional practices.

Dr. Felicello has presented at the NYS Athletic Administrator Conference, New York State Association of School Personnel Administrators Conference, New York State Curriculum for Advanced Technological Education Conference and at the OMEGA Institute.

Although Dr. Felicello is passionate about his career and improving our education system, his first priority is his family. He enjoys traveling and spending time with his wife Rebecca and 3 sons Justin (16), Andrew (15), and Scott (13).

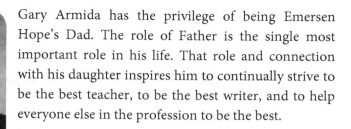 Gary Armida has the privilege of being Emersen Hope's Dad. The role of Father is the single most important role in his life. That role and connection with his daughter inspires him to continually strive to be the best teacher, to be the best writer, and to help everyone else in the profession to be the best.

Starting out as an eighth grade English Teacher, Armida has spent 15 of his 20 years as a classroom teacher at the high school level, teaching grades nine through eleven on all different levels and environments. His passion for writing extends to the classroom as his focus is to not only improve student writing, but to ignite a student's passion for the art of communication.

Over the past five years, Armida has assumed the role of English Department Coordinator. Through this role, he hopes to inspire colleagues to foster the love of the written word in their classrooms as well as help them create passionate, safe work environments for students. While the role is rewarding, the best parts of his work day are the three periods that he is in the classroom learning with his students.

Additionally, Armida works as an Adjunct Professor for Manhattanville College and The College of Mount St. Vincent, teaching graduate level courses focusing on literacy in secondary education.

Outside of the Education field, Armida has worked as a baseball writer. He's had work published by USA Today, Baseball Digest, Baseball Prospectus, Gotham Baseball Magazine, and for his own company, FullCountPitch Media, LLC.

GRATITUDE &
ACKNOWLEDGEMENTS

"Education is the most powerful weapon which you can use to change the world." ~ *Nelson Mandela*

We are forever grateful to Marlena Gross-Taylor and EduGladiators for the opportunity to write our first book. Thank you for giving our voice a platform in our quest to make schools better for kids. We could not have asked for a more kind, more progressive, and more innovative group of people to work with.

We would like to thank our "Voices from the field..." contributors, who gave their excellent, passionate words to add to our book. Our field is better because of them. Our lives are even more enriched not only because of our professional relationships, but because of their friendships.

Thank you to everyone in our field who has supported our work since we started the, The Teacher and The Admin website. Education stars such as Rick Wormeli, Jennifer Gonzalez, Evan Robb, Laura Robb, Richard Allan, and so many others have supported and inspired our work. Rick Wormeli even gave us the inspiration to write this book!

We thank you for taking the time and choosing to read our words. We realize that your time is valuable and there are many resources available. We are humbled that you chose our book. We hope that we were not only able to give you some practical tips to bring back to your district, but provide some hope that you are not in this alone and that what we do on a daily basis is vitally important.

THE **TEACHER** & THE **ADMIN**

We are grateful to all of our colleagues in the North Rockland Central School District. Many can say that they work in great places. But, we legitimately work in the best school district with the best people and the best kids.

Last, but certainly not least, we want to thank our families. Without their love, their support, and their understanding, none of this would ever be possible. And, quite frankly, none of it would be as meaningful.

MORE FROM
EDUGLADIATORS

Available everywhere books are sold.

The Future Is Now: Looking Back to Move Ahead
By Rachelle Dene Poth (@Rdene915)

If we are dedicated to facilitating the best futures for our students, we must be fully invested in lifelong learning and our personal and professional growth. In this book, the reader will hear from different educators, each sharing anecdotes and wisdom about becoming more connected, taking risks, and using failures and past experiences to help prepare for the future. Inspirational quotes appear throughout, prompting introspection and a call to action. A student also lends her perspective in a chapter, offering reflection from the other side of the classroom. When we strengthen ourselves as educators, we in turn empower others to do the same. Stronger together, we face whatever the future of learning will bring.

Bold Humility: Growing Students by Empowering Teachers
By David M. Schmittou (@daveschmittou)

It may seem like an oxymoron, but it is anything but that. BOLD humility is that secret "it" factor that we look for when trying to discover greatness. It is the balance of confidence and grace. It is wisdom coupled with vulnerability. It is the ability to bravely embrace what you know while being willing to seek support where you need it the most.

In this book, Dave takes a look at how educators can embrace BOLD humility to help tap into the greatness inside all of us. By sharing his own struggles coupled with his own successes, Dave paves a path that allows us all to walk away feeling empowered and ready to tackle the challenges that await us all.

My Pencil Made Me Do It: A Guide to Sketchnoting
By Carrie Baughcum (@HeckAwesome)

The pencil is a single tool that has the power to reset mindsets, enhance thinking, improve retention, recall, and comprehension, calm us and make us smile…all this from a pencil. My Pencil Made Me Do It is a unique, hands-on, create-to-connect and doodle-to-learn book that will have readers discovering powerful moments, learning the power behind visual thinking, and doodling to learn. Through honest perspective and creative insight, Carrie opens educators and students to visualize their thinking and their learning. While enabling them to experience how they can bring visual thinking into our world.

Champ For Kids
by Kelly Hoggard (@champforkids)

This book is for every teacher, no matter their level of experience. For seasoned veterans confidently navigating around the ring, find inspiration to continue to push on into the next round. For educators that feel as though every time they get on their feet, they are bruised and battered by another jab, make connections to this book to help develop a solid foundation towards becoming a champion. Finally to preservice educators standing outside the ring unsure if they have what it takes when the day comes to be tagged in, find the guidance and essentials needed to head into the ring. Champ For Kids inspires advocacy, going to the ropes for students, coaching them through mistakes so they land the TKO!

R.E.S.U.L.T.S.: Promoting Positive Behavior and Responsibility for Learning
by Krista Venza (@kristavenza) & Jon Treese (@jt2510)

R.E.S.U.L.T.S. is a book that provides applicable strategies for teaching students to make positive choices, take necessary action and promote growth. This book is an enjoyable mixture of inspiring stories and a framework that promotes positive behavior and responsibility for learning. From R.E.S.U.L.T.S., educators will feel empowered to make a difference in the lives of their students.

Made in the
USA
Middletown, DE